D1553072

DYING AND DIGNITY:

THE MEANING AND CONTROL
OF A PERSONAL DEATH

By

MELVIN J. KRANT, M.D.

CHARLES C THOMAS · PUBLISHER
Springfield · Illinois · U.S.A.

Published and Distributed Throughout the World by
CHARLES C THOMAS · PUBLISHER
Bannerstone House
301-327 East Lawrence Avenue, Springfield, Illinois, U.S.A.

© *1974, by* CHARLES C THOMAS · PUBLISHER
ISBN 0-398-02995-4 (cloth)
ISBN 0-398-02996-2 (paper)
Library of Congress Catalog Card Number: 73 13692

With THOMAS BOOKS *careful attention is given to all details of manufacturing and design. It is the Publisher's desire to present books that are satisfactory as to their physical qualities and artistic possibilities and appropriate for their particular use.* THOMAS BOOKS *will be true to those laws of quality that assure a good name and good will.*

Library of Congress Cataloging in Publication Data

Krant, Melvin J.
   Dying and dignity.

   1. Terminal care.   2. Physician and patient.   3. Death—Psychology.
I. Title. [DNLM: 1. Death.   2. Physician-Patient relations.   3. Terminal care.
BF789.D4 K89d 1974]
RC82.K7   362.1   73-13692
ISBN 0-398-02995-4
ISBN 0-398-02996-2 (pbk.)

Printed in the United States of America
H-2

PREFACE

DURING the past decade a great deal has been written on the topics of the dying patient and the meaning of death in Western society. These materials have been concentrated in professional journals, especially those dedicated to psychiatry, psychology, and sociology. General medical journals have carried some articles, devoted principally to questions of *truth-telling* and the physician's responsibility to the care of his dying patient. The general reading public has also been made aware of thoughts and discussions on the topics of dealth and dying via newspaper articles, magazines and several books.

A scholarly approach to the accumulated arguments and writings of this past decade, as well as antecedent years, would require an enormous publication. This has not been my intent at all. Instead, I have attempted to synthesize several ideas and concepts that relate to what I consider pertinent psychologic and sociologic information regarding the individual, his family, and the medical care system as they interrelate around the process of fatal illness and experience of dying. This synthesis is in fact highly personal, and is drawn from my experiences in the care of patients dying of cancer. Over these past several years, I have tried to relate the ideas, proposals, and pronouncements of the extensive literature on the subject with the personal problems that beset patients and their families, health care people and hospitals as institutions. My learnings have come from the care of patients and their families, as well as many hundreds of hours of discussion with medical and nursing students, with faculties of medical, law, theologic, and undergraduate teaching programs, with adult members of society taking evening adult education courses, and with friends and neighbors.

I have tried to understand what difficulties a person runs into, both intra-psychologically and in relationship to the society around him, when he develops a fatal illness, such as advanced cancer, and when he must deal with himself and significant others in moving towards

[v]

his death. I have struggled with an attempt to understand the word dignity, and how an individual in our times can feel himself dignified and in control of himself as he approaches his death. Certainly, much of his problem resides within himself as an individual, in relation to his concepts of person, strength, courage, concern for the other, and his belief in belonging to an order of things larger than himself, which perhaps we can call mankind. On the other hand, what society and institutions bring to the dying process exerts a considerable influence on the individual's concepts of himself and his personal dignity.

I have tried to write the book simply and in essay form, with a few pertinent references. The book is really not intended to be a manual of how to go about the process of dying, nor, as mentioned above, is it an attempt to be a scholarly tome, nor even a critique of modern society. It is intended to help individuals in general, families in general, and health care personnel in general, to look at some common tribulations that beset us all, and to ask if there is a way of enhancing the sense of dignity and control that all of us need throughout life if we are to feel a comfort and esteem with our individual lives. There are many individuals whose devotions, works, and conversations and guidance have helped in the writing of this essay. Dr. Cicely Saunders of London, England some years ago opened my eyes widely to what a physician and a hospice could do to give meaning to the end of one's life. Doctors Avery Weisman, Gerald Adler, Ned Cassem, Lee Johnston, Joseph Cohen and others in the Boston area have helped enormously to give perspective to my work with patients and families. To Mrs. Sandra Bertman I owe a debt for helping me clarify my ideas in writing. And to my wife, Mimi, I owe an enormous debt for her labors over the manuscript, and for her patience with me.

MELVIN J. KRANT, M.D.

CONTENTS

[vii]

DYING AND DIGNITY

CHAPTER I

SOME FACTS ABOUT
DYING TODAY

A PERSON WITH a fatal illness today is often caught up in a strange world of institutions and technology that may bring consolation in the form of battle against illness. Paradoxically this may cause him and his family considerable economic, psychologic and social pain and bewilderment. As he moves through that period of time in which he is both living with his disease and dying from it, much of the care offered is in scientific or technologic medical terms aimed specially at the disease process rather than at his suffering, as an individual. The patient becomes an individual with less and less control over his world and his destiny, and becomes increasingly caught up in current professional and institutional attitudes. Unable to derive a personal meaning to the end of his life, too many times a man or woman dies resigned, after a long, wearying illness, transmitting to those around him a sense of futility and despair. There is infrequently a peace at the end.

Such termination of a life is occurring, perhaps not unexpectedly, at a time when medical science has elaborated enormous potential for curing and foreshortening many of the serious health problems that beset man through past centuries. Perhaps this is the core of the problem. Such astonishing changes have occurred in the past seventy years in the overall pattern of diseases and death that the public meaning of personal death has become altered. As a population, modern Americans are much less initiated into the intimacy of dying and death than were previous generations, and the dying of a singular individual person with a fatal illness is a far more lonely, frightening and impersonal experience than in times gone by. An examination of some of the changes in our society over the present and past centuries, as well as changes in the evolving concepts of health care may shed some light on both the origin as well as the dimensions of this problem. It must be understood however, that we are not discussing all manners of dying. It is clear that a terrifying reality of senseless and violent death exists amongst us. We live with a spectre of the wastefulness of life, most penetratingly felt by the endless wars in Asia and effects of such conflict on the soldiers and families of America, Vietnam, Cambodia and elsewhere. To "waste" a person has become jargon in the military. Modern television communicates the "instance of" hurricane devastations in India; typhoons in Pakistan; slaughter in Nigeria and this is viewed as part of the larger "natural" human inheritance of death and destruction. And above us, at all times, hovers the potential insult of nuclear weaponry and catastrophic instant death, not only to each of us as singular people, but to the entire past lineage and future projection of men. We live in a time when aimless deaths from crime in the streets are mounting, and city streets are turning into vacant cement alleyways at night. We have become accustomed to hearing the call to violence preached in revolution and have the feeling that bloodletting is now a prayer to improve loving man.

Death is all about us in accidents, in the drug scene, in alcoholism, in murder and in suicide. Intellectually we may express horror at it all, but in reality it would seem that all this death is too distant and *other person* for our gut to be truly upset, unless it is we who are personally involved. Most of us go on living in our accustomed style, perhaps a bit uncomfortable, but as if there really was little choice.

Despite the open visibility of violent and accidental death, there has been a vacuum in attempts to understand and interact with the personal meaning in a personal death resulting from a natural or disease process. There seems to be an absence of style or knowledge as to how an ill person should handle his dying, and people appear to be uncertain as to how they should act in the face of the slow dying of a loved one. A question of dignity and of the right to dignity in dying is frequently raised, and criticisms are heard that medical technology dominates the ending of human life by extending biologic life when the human life has ceased. An impersonal professional style seems to have replaced meaningful human interaction at the time of a man's dying and during the period of grief and mourning of his survivors. Without a manner or a style, the dying individual seems to have so little control over the mechanics and design of his dying. The responsibility for dying has fallen to the health professionals—the physician, the nurse and the technician. They have become the critical decision-makers around issues of dying while the patient, his family and the ministry are relegated to secondary positions. It would appear that the individual death no longer belongs to the individual life.

This is not to imply that thinkers, philosophers, poets and artists have not struggled with the issue of the meaning of death in modern times. The need to make sense of death, especially in human or humanistic terms, has grown considerably as the consolations of religion and immortality have become less acceptable. A search for the personal dimensions of dying has resulted in angry accusations as to the absurdity of life on one hand and on the other, in intense declarations that since there is nothing to life but its immediate existence, one must seize the moment.[1] The psychologically oriented modern social critic has described death as a post-Christian, twentieth century labor, an awesome phenomenon divested of direct public examination and thus distorted into pornography.[2] Pornography in this sense is defined as a public peeking into a common human circumstance, of which our society does not allow natural visibility. Whatever the tack, in attempts to explain the philosophical dimensions of death in the holocaust-ridden twentieth century western world, the loneliness and gracelessness of modern man constantly emerges, more than a bit bewildered by the constant presence of something he appears eager to avoid.

The purpose of this writing is not to deal with all the ramifications of death and dying. I wish to focus on the nature of the dying experience for a person who has a fatal illness intrude into his existence. For such an individual, it is not merely in abstracted philosophic principles that he is pained, but in those day-by-day events that characterize his living as he moves towards death. The primary and essential question I wish to raise is whether a person's death truly belongs to him as part of a personal life that belongs to him, or not. The answer would appear undeniably in the negative, namely that most people with fatal illness do not die in the assurance that their deaths belong to them as meaningful summations of their lives.

As we seek for some explanation of this phenomenon of impersonal or resigned death, we will have to accept the fact that probably no one answer suffices; and perhaps not even the collective explanations from the research and observations of sociologists, psychologists, anthropologists and other similar students of men and society are sufficiently elucidating. Nevertheless, there are certain phenomena that we can understand and even a dusting of insight is better than a "that's how it is" shrug.

Probably the most impressive statistical alteration in our time which tends to make personal death less visible and meaningful and controllable has been the change in American life expectancy. In the United States today, the average life expectancy for white (Caucasian) men is 72.5 years and for white women, 75 years. What this means is that a child born today can expect to live at least to these figures, depending on his or her sex. For many, additional years into the late 70's, 80's and even 90's will not be exceptional. If we compare this figure, the average life expectancy, with some figures from the recent and distant past, the alteration in individual expected survival, estimating this figure in years of life from the days of birth, is hardly anything but remarkable. At the turn of the century the average survival time for both sexes was approximately only 47 years. This figure can be compared with the average survival times in mid-nineteenth-century England where by best estimates, the average expectancy was about 41 years. For further comparison, figures have been estimated as to average life survival in Roman times of 2,000 years ago, when it would appear that the average was 22 years. Very rough estimations of average survival rates in still more ancient times, as in pre-laterate societies, give us figures of about 18 years.[3]

These remarkable changes, especially in the last 150 years, have reflected the sharp decline in mortality for the child and young adult, especially the child-bearing woman. At the turn of this century in America, 53 percent of all recorded deaths were in children under the ages of 15, at a time when people of this age bracket were registered as 34 percent of the entire population. In that same time period, the beginning of the twentieth century, people over the ages of 65 were only 4 percent of the total population and contributed 17 percent of the deaths in the overall mortality statistics. By the end of the 1960's, these figures were sharply altered. The overall population in the United States has grown from 40 million to 200 million and the number of people over 65 are now 9 percent of the total. However of all the deaths in the United States, two thirds or 67 percent were found in this age bracket while less than one third of all deaths were in the younger age groups. Thus dying has become virtually the province of the older person. This dramatic reversal of mortality rates from young to old reflects the considerable engineering, biologic and medical advances of the past hundred years. Young people still die of congenital malformations, accidents and poisonings. Childhood cancer still takes a toll, but progress in the twentieth century has diminished this toll so that comparatively, only a few families now suffer the death of a child. The relative paucity of childhood deaths, associated as this phenomena is with smaller households of generally fewer children per family unit, has resulted in an absence of the "presence" of a young death for the young family. Such an absence is welcomed indeed.

Of the two million deaths in this country yearly, nearly 1.5 million of them are over the age of 65, although the maximum years lived by any one individual has changed little if at all, from older days. It is the older citizen who not only dies, but who has become part of a considerably altered social and economic environment from times past. The elderly no longer live among the young with a sense of intimacy and belonging as they did in the past. A considerable amount of social separation has developed with the old living apart from the young. The dying and death of the elderly frequently occurs at a distance from the home of the young, who seldom participate in the care of the sick individual or in the good-bye takings of family members. Children may learn of the death of a beloved grandparent but infrequently attend the events of the dying itself.

Sociologists have painted this social separation in rather vivid terms and there are not many who are not acquainted with descriptions such as nuclear families, procreative families, extended families, urban shifts, mobile families and the like.

In the rural farm society, working of the land for the survival of all members demanded a family stability, a rootedness and an inter-generational continuity. Families labored together and several generations were usually housed under one roof. Daughters might leave for other farms through marriage, sons might occasionally go off to develop new lands, but each would soon reorganize another integrated, multigenerational unit. Men lived and died on property that was theirs, in full participation with the family group and in command of available resources. The elders in the family group were in their own homes when they died. It was rare for any one individual to be too independent when proximity in living and the demands for co-ordinated group performance limited personal choice and defined the individual in relation to the kinship formula. Education was frequently limited to the knowledge of the land system and the kin group.

In such an intergenerational, land-based system, death was commonly and frequently in the home, be it of animals for slaughter and food, or of people through accident, through aging or through sickness. The experiences were clearly visible to the child and adult. Few persons were born or died in hospitals, and attending to the most personal needs of the sick and dying were the natural responsibilities of young and old. Burials were family affairs and graves were dug on the family land, or the dead were buried in community churchyards where entire families and communities not only attended, but walked freely among the stones of others dead and buried. Children were not protected or sheltered. That death was more intimate to life is not to imply that one shred of the fearful awesomeness of death was diminished. Proximity however, frequently brings a necessity to deal with death on one level or another, and orders some rehearsing of one's personal approach to dying.

The modern industrial and technological society, urban based as it is, results in quite the opposite experience for young and old. The small nuclear family is an appropriate answer to the requirements of large, widely distributed industries where shifts of personnel from one city to another, is common. Education implies perfecting technical and scientific skills and understanding. With the enormity of new knowledge generated each year, education is no longer an intra-family phenomenon, but is institutionalized away from home. Young people must make choices early in life for professionalized education and rapidly move out to find themselves and to create new nuclear organizations. Large homes are no longer needed and smaller homes and apartments are now built. Parents are not long depended upon for economics, education, decision-making and the like. The older citizen is forced to accept a discontinuity from the role of parent to the role of independent older citizen. Frequently the reverse occurs, and older people become dependent upon their children for housing, economics and decision-making, a dependency role that most older citizens in our society loathe. Older citizens in urban areas often select and prefer to live alone and independently even though the price for this independence may be loneliness (despite the occasional telephone call and visit), economic deprivation, nonmobility (especially with the terror of the streets at night) and stagnation. Even when the fortunate and successful elderly move to sunny, warm climates and find pleasure and ease in living, the effect is to promote a generation separation that effectively keeps the young from interacting with the nature of aging, illness and dying.

The result is a recent and new dimension for death, namely its nonvisibility due to rearranged social forces. It is the elderly who mostly die in our time, but they are not among the rest of the population. Seldom in control of the family's destiny, seldom in close proximity to the emotional dependence of children and grandchildren, frequently lagging behind in the modern world's parades of knowledge and strength, their dislocation from life itself is added to by the propagation of retirement colonies in warm climates and old age homes in the cities. Some choose to be out of sight this way; others are forced to be. Either way, the elderly are frequently out of sight, especially when they die. This emphasis on segregation, in chronological terms, drives a certain naturalness of dying and death out of focus for younger people. Dying becomes alien to life and frightening to conceptualize.

As a corollary but of significant social, educational and personal importance, is the fact that men no longer die in their homes in the midst of their families and possessions. They now die in institutions, prinicipally hospitals, extended care facilities and nursing homes. At the turn of the century in cities such at Baltimore and San Francisco,

75 to 80 percent of deaths took place at home. Today quite the reverse holds, especially in the cities where more than 75 percent of deaths are recorded in institutions.[4] For the many individuals who die in hospitals, the end of their lives come under the control of a staff of professionals who may be more concerned with certain biologic and physiologic events than with the wholeness of their human charges. The fright, impotence, and loneliness of the patient is seldom attended to although his body fluids, temperature and blood pressure are carefully monitored. While fear and loneliness are difficult to attend to, their character becomes increasingly profound when those in the immediate vicinity appear uninterested or helpless themselves in administering appropriate aid. The modern medical staff seems to be untrained to deal in these human perspectives and the dying person himself is in a position of weakness, not strength, in controlling events in his environment.

Most institutions, as hospitals, extended care facilities or nursing homes, function poorly in regard to the dying individual. Hospitals especially (but the same holds for nursing homes) operate to prevent individuals from exercising control of their limited environments and at the same time, behave as if death were illegitimate or an abomination.[5] Hospitals are frequently anxious to make death and dying invisible to the living.[6] If a patient is in a two-, or a four-bed room or larger and his condition indicates to the medical staff that death is near, he is frequently moved to a private room so that other patients and their visitors will not have to see death come. Perhaps it is also reasoned that the staff will be checking the patient frequently, there may be many relatives around and thus add to the disturbance of other patients. But the need to protect others from seeing death at first hand is a very potent reason for such privacy. When a death occurs, the hospital policy is to keep the event invisible as though visibility would frighten other patients and be interpreted as an undermining of the curative or rehabilitative power of modern medicine. Sometimes one has the feeling that hospitals wish to impart the image of happy places where only "good" and "pleasant" things occur. At any rate, the dead body is usually transported to the morgue after being trussed and placed in an appropriate shroud, but only after the doors to other patients' rooms are closed, visitors are cleared from the corridors, and a special elevator is commandeered. Everyone in the ward knows, but no one talks about it.

The dying patient is frequently in an intensive care unit with much bewildering equipment hooked into him, with his family in the corridor and allowed entrance for short intervals only. Young children are seldom present. They are kept away, even if the dying individual might wish them near.

Not long ago as I was leaving the lobby of a major Boston hospital, the receptionist stopped a young boy of about twelve years. She was a kindly looking woman in her fifties, I would judge. When asked where he was going, the boy replied, "to see my grandmother." He was told that children were not allowed visiting privileges. As things turned out however, his grandmother was an employee and not a patient, and she was summoned.

I approached the receptionist a moment later and asked what would have happened if the boy's grandmother had been a patient and perhaps dying. "He absolutely could not go in!" But supposing his grandmother was requesting him? "She wouldn't have a chance at all to see him." As I pursued this dialogue, anxious to know why, who made the rules, and what did the receptionist think of such regulations, all that I could get back was, "I don't make the rules, I have my orders," and, "that's how it is." There was nothing really brutal or inhuman about this lady. On the contrary, her manner was soft, kind, even somewhat maternal. She was just caught up in the controlling hospital system designed to protect the child, I suppose, from the realities of life and death. Perhaps that judgment is too harsh. Perhaps a twelve-year-old child might disrupt hospital efficiency and is excluded for that reason. If so, it is a poor reason indeed.

Institutional dying is frequently devoid of the concept of "natural" death, especially if the patient is less than elderly. Scientific medicine demands that each death have a cause and such causes, of course, are called diseases. The very core of modern medicine is an understanding of the biologic nature of disease. The problem for the dying patient is that he is often caught up in an institutional activity that is attempting to alter the nature of his disease right up to the last possible moment. The advantages offered to the person with a fatal illness by such biological pursuits in the early and perhaps middle stages of his illness, are turned into disadvantages at the end of the illness, when a surcease of vigorous attack seems indicated and a gentility and peacefulness is desired. Defining death as the ravaging of a disease creates an unrelentless attack on the disease, with the coming of death as inappropriate. Institutions seldom allow for truly peaceful endings. The patient is forced into the role of combatant to the end.

Institutional practices also promote specialization as a particular outgrowth of the professionalization of knowledge. The accumulation of factual material regarding disease and biology has promoted the development of professionals and specialists. As a nation, we seem to be particularly vulnerable to the expertise of professionals. This perhaps, as part of our belief that all things in life are based on rational, measurable parameters. We now rely minimally on self-determined ways of answering problems. We are thus apt to feel uncomfortably helpless to reject offered professional advice, even when we do not agree with it. It is not often that we can shoulder the responsibility for self-determined action when a professional person has insisted that the problem be solved his way. The professional often has institutional back-up for his arena of action, and the persuasion of institution and professional together is enormous. We often feel small and ineffectual when confronting the significance of institutions and professionals. People often simply resign themselves to these powers, often with a helpless or hopeless attitude when they feel impotent to act on their own behalf. Despair rather than peace ensues. We do not feel safe without the professional, but often feel helpless to challenge what is being done.

This particular force to bend to the wisdom of the professional is not only for protection, but also because of an expectancy that is both rational and fantasy-like. The enormous growth of technologic capability has produced an expectancy that life's problems are now solvable by the application of scientific knowledge and principals. The sick patient frequently struggles with this expectancy that the answer to his disease problem is available somewhere. Frightened of his illness, he often expects his modern-day doctor to either have the answer, or to be able to send him somewhere where the answer resides. Men have always searched for miraculous answers to the tragic events of life. While at one time mystics and soothsayers offered hope, the search is now predominantly through modern medicine. In some ways, we have been led to believe that death, especially death prior to some exceedingly old age, might never have to be if only we apply existing technology and knowledge appropriately. The patient with a fatal illness, or his family, often seems to be acting as though his particular salvation and rescue rests in the hands of the medical profession. In large part, this attitude reflects the national energies invested in conquering diseases, such as cancer (with news coverage of breakthroughs actual or imminent, and the elaboration of technology as a resource for curing, in such forms as huge radiation treatment centers). With all this effort and publicity, an actual death due to illness is frequently treated as suspect or illegitimate, quite out of keeping with expectancy.

The eradication of so much death from childhood and young adult years and the promise of technology and research, have become conditions for almost demanding an end to death. Immorality groups have appeared, concerning themselves not with the universal and time-immemorial arguments and dreams of the human soul, but with immortality today for living men, a corporeal immortality in which death is not just indefinitely postponed, but eradicated. The basic thematic quotation of *The Immortality Newsletter,* a new publication originating in California is, "Death is an imposition on the human race and no longer acceptable." [7] A number of publications have appeared insisting that the end of death is within man's potential. To vitalize this position, believers are taking the bodies of the dead and freezing them in a liquid nitrogen capsule in order to preserve flesh, so that the individual can be revived in some future time when medicine will have a cure for the illness that brought death. The bodies frozen today in a scheme called Cryonics, have died recently. The December, 1970 issue of *The Immortality Newsletter* indicated that the fourteenth patient had been so treated, a Mrs. M.H., a 55-year-old victim of cancer. The body is stored in California and "will remain in anabiosis until a cure for cancer has been discovered and successfully established, whereupon she will, hopefully, be revived and treated." [7] The future appears to hold an option for freezing and preservation before death has occurred. Preservation of intact bodies by freezing is certainly possible, and the technology to accomplish this already exists, although the possibility for revival back to normal in the sense of brain and other tissue recovery, is highly in doubt. While there does exist this marginal effort to deny death its due, I cannot be certain that such action brings consolation to the dying. Certainly if one is convinced that he is not really dying in his death, but will be returned, there is almost a religious salvation in such conviction. But such belief in technology and corporeal immortality is rare.

In today's world of fatal illness and dying, as it is in the world of aging, the modern citizen finds himself in an uncomfortable position. With few of the older traditional supports such as religion, home, family, community and land to nourish him, he has become dependent on professionals and institutions to minister to his needs. Successful as they are, the professionals and the institutions seem more concerned with disease and biology than with human meaning. Ideas and concepts such as self-worth, dignity and self-control are not part of the institutionalized response to fatal illness. There is a scarcity of attention paid to the meaning of suffering on human terms, and little search for helping the dying find meaning and dignity to their lives. For the fatally ill, disease has become synonymous with biology. Trust and faith in a safe and understanding personal caring environment has slipped away as an essential in compassionate response to suffering. The modern citizen, sheltered from visible death most of his life, has been so unprepared to think about death as a part of his life and has been so unrehearsed in the interaction with styles of dying, that he feels helpless, lost and frequently overdependent on the powerful professionals. He comes to his dying confused, angry and in many ways, unprepared. He finds that his dying is not under his control, but under the control of others.

[1]Choron, Jacques: *Death and Western Thought*. New York, Collier Books. An analysis of many differing philosophical positions in regard to the meaning of death for modern European and American man.
[2]Gorer, Geoffrey: *Death, Grief and Mourning*. Garden City, N.Y. Doubleday, 1965. A study of contemporary society.
[3]Lerner, Monroe: When, why and where people die. In Brim, O.G., Jr., Freeman, H.E., Levine, S., and Scotch, N.I.A. (Eds.): *The Dying Patient*. New York, Russell Sage Foundation, 1970.

[4]Public Health Service: *Vital Statistics of the United States, 1958.* Washington, D.C., U.S. Government Printing Offiice, 1960, Vol. II, Table 57.

[5]Glaser, Barney G., Strauss, Anselm, L.: *Awareness of Dying.* Chicago, Aldine, 1965. The authors present an extended set of observations in the function of the modern American hospital and the associated medical and nursing staffs in regard to communication with the dying person.

[6]Sudnow, David: *Passing On: The Social Organization of Dying.* Englewood Cliffs, N.J., Prentice-Hall, 1967.

[7]Otto, A. Stuart (Ed.): *The Immortality Newsletter.* December, 1970.

CHAPTER II

FEARS REGARDING DEATH

Is IT POSSIBLE to talk of controlling the manner of one's death, or is the concept of death so fearful and so alien that most of us can only flee from the face of death, or let death conquer without our active participation with it. Certainly there is fear when we think or talk of death, but what is it that we do fear? Can we elucidate the origin and strength of death fears? Are there other descriptive terms that might do more justice to that which we feel when we allow ourselves to talk of death abstractly? And are these feelings innate and genetic? That is, do they exist because they are an essential quality that is inherent in being a human being? If not, do these feelings emerge from cultural or social teachings? Are there societies of men where death fears do not exist or, if some fear or concern is universal, are there societies where the *dealings* with death overcome fear, allowing for significantly less anxiety and less of a feeling of aloneness than we know exists in western culture?

It is safe to begin with the assumption that there certainly is a fear of death and that this fear has an essential utilitarian aspect in protecting life. "You can get killed doing that" or, "I nearly died lifting that bundle" are simple phrases illustrating the sense of concern and caution for individual life that protects us from exposing ourselves to senseless annihilation. We teach caution to our children with fire, with streets, with windows, with stairs, in order to avoid accidents periling health and life. Infants and young children appear to have an absence of appreciable fear in regard to their environment and parents must be constantly alert to the potential devastation in a child's striving to explore his expanding world. In this regard, the very survival of a species depends upon the innate characteristics of a drive to live and an avoidance of accidental death, especially in early and procreative years. Almost all mammalian offspring, and man in particular, are critically weak, vulnerable and helpless and need education and guidance to protect against injury and death. Does this very drive to defend life carry with it the penalty of an extended fear of death? Does a fear that was useful for survival in the early and growing years as well as in the adult years become a barrier towards a peaceful ending of life when death is close by? We cannot answer for sure, but nature frequently provides man with the resources for change and adaptability, and a once useful fear could well be discarded at a critical time if educational, psychologic and social messages have not complicated matters.

If there is a genetic death fear, then teasing out this "inborn" aspect from the complicated and learned intellectual and social milieu of the human life would be difficult at best, if not impossible. To complicate matters, there may well be a drive towards death that Freud and other psychoanalysts have vaguely described and discussed. For some in the psychoanalytic field, human actions that are risky and are a challenge to life or limb are explanable as a movement towards thanatos, a drive, instinctively, in the human towards mortality. The possibility of a thanatotrophic movement in the human psyche is too complicated a discourse for our purposes and remains more theoretical than confirmed, but it is probably safe to conclude that if such a drive exists, it does not appear to have a calming effect in matters concerning death for most people in the western world.[1,2]

We can ask if the protecting fear just mentioned is the same as an abstracted generalized fear of death? Again, it is hard to be certain. Modern psychoanalytic argument seems to presume that the fear of death is a psychologic process that springs either from an inner tension that is innate in the newborn child, or is quickly derived in the world of the developing child. One theoretical assumption is that the fear of death is secondary to the anxieties of abandonment and separation, and the anxieties of castration. In this context, the young child is perceived as quickly recognizing, shortly after birth, that he or she is dependent on parents, but essentially the mother, for those nutrients and protection that insure continuing life. This infantile awareness imposes a great psychologic dependency which is marked by a concern for the possibility of abandonment or separation. In the case of the latter, death would ensue from lack of the nutrients supplied by the mother. The death fear thus interrelates to maternal dependency. The possibility of abandonment registers in the unconscious and from this, a more permanent anxiety over death eventuates and persists into adult life.[3]

Carried to a further development dependency relations, abandonment and separation anxieties and death fear become interwoven in adult life so that abandonment, seen as loneliness or aloneness, is equated with death and death in turn, is equated with abandonment, aloneness, isolation. A fear of the dark is intimately associated, for to the child, nighttime and the dark are fearful because mother is out of sight. She is not able to be seen even if there. Children who develop a deep fear of the dark are apt to become adults who interpret the dark, the night and death as a unity. Certainly our language frequently speaks of the dark, the black, the night, as death images. Dying people tend to dislike, if not outrightly fear, the dark, perhaps as an unbearable reminder of childhood separation from mother.

Death is also frequently thought of as punishment, or in fact, feared as punishment. In psychoanalytic terms, castration theory gives the parent, especially the father, the image of a furious, punishing figure who will symbolically kill his son for sexually coveting father's most desired possession, namely mother. Since the male child is not only deeply dependent on the mother for nutrient and protection, but also may well see her as his first sexual exciter, fear of the reprisal from father for such forbidden lusting is said to be the equivalent of fear of death. Further, castration is not only related to a symbolic personal death, but it is also the death of an individual's procreative capability. The need to see oneself as immortal through the seed may well be another human characteristic, and castration effectively destroys this potential. Death is thus equated with punishment for evil thoughts and sin, producing guilt feelings and death-as-punishment images in adulthood.

There is another body of psychoanalytic thought that tends to somewhat reverse the derivative order, ranking fear of death as primary and separation anxiety and castration, or oedipal complex as secondary. This latter view is also charged with the concept that the mother may well be a damaging, punitive, annihilating figure, disliking her offspring and threatening him with death through the threat of withdrawing love, and thus nutrient, from the child.[3]

While most people would immediately deny the possibility that parents, especially mothers, harbor death wishes for their children, it is astonishing how often, in little ways, such messages in the form of threats of abandonment, are communicated to children. On one recent trip, I watched three different mothers threaten their children with abandonment at airports. The women were in a rush to get somewhere and their little children, three or four years old, were lagging behind. In three completely separate events they turned to their children and shouted "good-bye" or "we're leaving you", in an attempt to force their children to catch up with them. As innocent as the gesture may appear, the applied threat to abandon if the child does not obey must be terrifying to a youngster.

In either of these psychoanalytic views, death fears are easily related to childhood experiences in which threats to survival, primary or secondary, result in permanent psychological scars that make the fear of death in adulthood not only a useful, life-protecting tool, but a destructive, intimidating psychosis-neurosis creator, responsible for mental and social disturbance.

In this light, it is instructive to review some of the childhood rhymes, fables, myths and tales, for they appear to serve dual functions. In one way they expose many death and separation fears that children possess by projecting them onto a distant character and a distant setting, and allow the child to exteriorize or project inner psychologic pressure. On the other hand, they tend to demonstrate that these terrible fears and concerns can be mastered by agility, cleverness, chance or just goodness, so that the child can control the situation and need not fear permanently.

The Snow White tale clearly describes the female competitive conflict between the child and a maternal figure over the issue of beauty. Characteristically, as in many such tales, the maternal person is a stepmother, for it would appear that to ascribe ultimate cruelty and malignity to a natural mother would be too much for any culture to tolerate. Snow White's competitive beauty is more than her step-

mother can bear, and the latter resorts to extraordinary efforts including conspiratorial interweavings with black magic for the annihilation of the princess. That Snow White does not yield to death but
instead sleeps to be awakened by a wandering Prince Charming who
loves only her, not only fulfills the child (adult) fantasy for ultimate
rescue and immortality, but demonstrates that beauty and goodness
will win out and be rewarded by the love of a magnificent man.
An extraordinary dimension of this fable is the neutrality and virtual
absence of the father, either as a casual or a consequential agent (although one might say that the Prince and the father are one). Father's
benignity is assured by his absence, and he remains nonindicted and
pure in this mother-daughter conflict that motivates the passion of
the tale.

   The Hansel and Gretel story also invites terror by the visualization
of the selfishness and lovelessness of a stepmother who abandons her
children in the woods in order to preserve nutrient essential for her
own life. A wicked witch is cast in the role of provider (another
maternal figure) but merely for the sake of fattening the children
for ultimate consumption. Fantasy-rescue provides the out, but this
time through the childrens' cleverness and agility. Again father is cast
in a loving but ineffectual role, destitute at his loss of children, rejoic-
ing at their return, but essentially incapable of ameliorating the inherent mother-child competition.

   The story of Jack and the Beanstalk takes clear account of the
problems faced in coveting father's possessions. The great Giant,
slobbering in his excesses, mutters the "fe-fie-fo-fum" tune, im-
precating the child Jack to his death (again, by the way, by being
eaten). Jack, by stealing the Giant's fondest possessions, the hen
that lays the golden eggs and the singing harp (both accommodating,
feminine delight-givers), is pursued into death by this huge, hulking
monster, only to rescue himself by wit and thus gain the happiness of
mother (who of course, in being widowed, allows Jack full domi-
nance). The Giant's wife is depicted as kindly, maternal, protective,
and it is the Giant who harbors the competitive evil, hoarding the
treasures for himself.

   One of the most profound tales embodying the life-giving and life-
taking submissiveness is the biblical story of the potential sacrifice of

Isaac by the patriarch Abraham. Obeying the commandment of God, Abraham takes his beloved son and makes ready to slaughter him as sacrifice to the wishes of the Almighty. Only a last minute reprieve allows the substitution of a ram for the son. If we allow for a possible interpretation of this tale as the projected psychological description of the wish for infanticide (unbearable to accept as inherently dynamic in the role of paternity and therefore projected out as a response to an awe-majestic God), it is not difficult to sense the helpless fear of the child before the potency of the father.[4]

As we briefly examine western religions, it is obvious that the sense of retribution and punishment, inherent in feelings of guilt and self-blame, has been astutely incorporated into the texts of the faith. The Old Testament is filled with tales of God's wrath and devastating vengeance on man for ill-doing. The story of Noah and the Ark demonstrates the value of piety and God's interest in continuity, but also of course, we are shown the enormous punitive capacity against all but the selected few. The story of Lot and the City of Gomorrah gives further strength to the vindicating nature of God. Even for the relatively minor infraction of looking back, a good and virtuous woman is turned to a pilar of salt while on her walk to salvation. The Christian Church not only perpetuated the crime, guilt and punishment theme, but created a massive heaven-hell after-life vision, where the rewards or punishments for the behavior in the earth-bound life would be bestowed.

Although certainly no longer an intensely viable doctrine for the modern, earthy intellectual, the doctrinal implications of original sin and punishment still exert a hold on the thoughts of many people, especially the older generation. Hell may be nothing more, according to the analysts, than a psychologic projection of man's eternal need for punishment, originating in a guilty subconscious. But subtle, and even sometimes obvious, enforcing pressure through society and education, frequently reinforces the not-too-well-articulated concepts of hell, and such fearful thoughts linger as a discomforting uncertainty that may jeopardize peaceful days for many. It is really not essential for us to debate whether few or many people feel that they exist predestined for grace or for damnation. The organic principle of sin, and of judgment and punishment, carries an overt or implied threat that can make one fearful about death. Even if there is the possibility of forgiveness, working one's way into eternal grace carries the implied possibility of failure to accomplish foregiveness. Once formed within the mind, these interpretations of heaven or hell seem beyond rational argument, and therefore are not available for intellectualization. If one feels the weight of sin and evil, the interstices and dark recesses of the fearful mind casts at least a mild-though-moldy uncertainty at what death threatens. As already stated, I would not care to argue as to the frequency of such thoughts in people. I'm sure no statistics exist, but I have seen uncertainty frequently in people who claim to be nonreligious, and there seems little doubt that once the kernel is implanted in the soul of the young, it has enormous staying power even if dormant (especially if allowed to remain unexposed). The problem is amplified in modern society, where an enormous reliance exists on the rational and the measurable to explain our lives. The pageantry, the rituals and the rites once directed through religion or culture in order to expose and ameliorate such inner psychologic pressures and fears, have been either diminished or abandoned entirely, leaving these seeds of fear if once implanted, to lie intestate and unchallenged.

In today's young and exuberant generation, many grow up unexposed to the teaching of doctrinal sin, judgment, punishment or expiation. It is not part of the modern education for life. The mystical and the nonrational seems to have become a minor part of whatever is left of religion. The religious attitude appears now more toward earth-bound reflections of morals, good deeds, politics, race and the like, and God speaks the language of the every day. In this state, death is argued only in the materialistic and humanistic sense. What is known of man is measurable in terms of his functional parts, and so with death comes nothingness. All is finite. As hell is obliterated, so is heaven. This may be more terrifying than ever, for if all that describes man does so only in his finiteness, then the surrendering of this immediate world implies total extinction. The consolations of rational philosophy barely help many in facing this existentialistic absurdity, the sense of total annihilation. Ignace Lepp, in his reflections on the mysteries of death, relates an incident which so well captures this overwhelming abomination, extinction.

The incident occurred at a conference held in Bruges, Belgium in 1964. A symposium had convened to discuss the ideas of Tielhard de Chardin, a French 20th-century philosopher and theologian who has had an especial impact on modern thinking in areas of human destiny. It is not possible to describe adequately de Chardin's concepts of human spirituality in a few words, but suffice to say, his ideas are positive, exuberant and expansive, highly optimistic. An eminent politician rose at the end of the symposium to say:

> your Tielhardian optimism in all of its cosmic and communitarian aspects is very attractive, but it neglects a fundamental fact, namely that we are all mortal. As soon as I mentally contemplate on my own death I feel alone and abandoned, the prey of anguish. The essential problem for me then becomes not what the state of the universe or humanity will be in 1,000 years, but what awaits me personally.[5]

Fear of death may well have become magnified as those once existing forces that attempted to give meaning to death and thus to life, have disintegrated. For the Christian believer of the distant past, the day of death was the day of the new life. Fundamental Catholic tradition still holds that the moment of death is *deus natalis,* the rebirth into eternal life. Modern Protestant groups and Jews as well, are much more timid regarding the dynamic virtues of an afterlife or anything resembling not just benignity toward death, but positive joy with death. The notion of death as a time of reunion with lost loved ones has become too childish a notion for a serious modern adult to consider.

Nonreligious consolations for the fear of death have probably existed since the beginning of man's existence on this earth.[6] The concerns of modern man about death are certainly not new. Since recorded history men have struggled to make sense of death. Classical Greek rational thought of 2,000 years ago struggled with these issues and a number of philosophies evolved such as The Epicurian, The Stoical and The Sophist. In a most materialistic pronouncement, Euripides held forth the consolation, "where I am, death is not, and where death is, I am not; therefore, there is no reason to worry of death." Since men and death could not be in the same place at the same time in the sense that once dead, man could not think about death, Euripides could therefore argue that any concern was illogical,

elicited the humble answer "a poor mortal sinner," at which point the gate opened and the cortege proceeded within. Equality through death may have been a compensatory theme in an older Christian world, but it holds little supportive help for today's secular living.

The ways of extinct, primitive and/or more agrarian cultures were quite different. In many primitive, preliterate societies and cultures, death and fertility were made the balancing arms around the fulcrum of life. Such societies were intimately concerned with the coordination, harmony and well-being of the entire community, and individuals as such were less of a concern. For the Aztecs in older Mexico, life only justified itself when realized in death, for death was the transfiguration and transcendence of life.[11] To the Aztec as well as to the Christian of another era, life was a transition, a profound way of participating in the continuous regeneration of the creative force, and sacrifice in blood was as a positive virtue in symbolizing utter belief in commonality and regeneration. Actual sacrificial practices seem barbaric to modern man for in the democratic sense, each death belongs to a particular life as a fact and not as a symbol. In the evolution of such democratic principles the "belonging" of life and death to the larger community of men has been indicted and has degenerated, together with the symbolic acts of the sacrifice.

A serious existential concern regarding dying and death in the modern, secular world is the fear of losing one's life before it can be fulfilled. That word "fufilled" has a highly personal tone to it. It may matter little what visible accomplishments the individual has actually made, for fulfillment is one's perception of oneself. Even without the fear of overt punishment, many dying patients appear to be quite concerned, even fearful, as to whether there has been any true goodness or value in their past days. At times, such concern can be quite intense, implying a considerable amount of guilt or doubt that the life may not have lived up to an expected, idealized or imagined level of behavior.

Death is thus feared for it will catch people short of time to make amends and correct wrongs, to put life into order. This feeling of an incompleted life may not be as much a fear as it is a resentment. Perhaps both emotions, fear and resentment, operate together. The fear, if it exists, may not be for the end of life, and resentment, in such cases, is not a rationalization for the fear of death itself. The fear, or resentment, is for a wasted, unfulfilled life, a life of promises and not completions. Many persons seem to act in life as if they could postpone their true, singular fulfillment, waiting until some later moment to really begin living. The nearness of death catches them short.

The concept of self-fulfillment implies a strong personal ego, one that is comfortable with its identity, and feels a sense of self-esteem. In this regard it is the self-esteem that is critical, the inwardly directed security that is unrelated to any particular event or deed, but is dependent on an inner feeling that one is well with his world and has been well with his past.[12] Self-esteem is a life's endeavor, a meaningful working-through of the person with his particular time, space, culture and history, to allow a sense of inner confidence and an easy interaction with others. Self-fulfillment is difficult at best to acquire in a rootless, mobile, competitive, machine-oriented world, and age by itself is no guarantee of fulfillment. There may be some solace in staying alive into the elderly years, with the anticipation that the full cycle of life will be completed as the years advance. The older a person is the easier it supposedly is to accept death as the natural ending of life. But it is not uncommon for people in their sixties and seventies to view approaching death as premature, robbing them of an opportunity to truly live.

The feelings of self-worth are critical in life, but they are equally so in dying. Death may be welcomed for some as a resignation from a burdensome life. In this regard, death may not be seen as fear, although in that conclusion of resignation, rests a condemning sorrow for the emptiness and hollowness of the life preexisting. The dying of an elderly, lonely, bewildered person may well be welcomed in the resignation of a badly plagued life. Such resignation is painful in its brutal portrayal of disappointments, vitiations and denials of the self that didn't make it in life.

In the same context, the young may die with a sense of peace and fullness, despite our abstract ethical horror at the abbreviation of life before some preconceived "completion" has occurred. In a romantic way, the testing of life's bitterness was avoided. Romanticization of young dying was common in the centuries past. Tuberculosis was the grim stalker of the aesthetic young, and poets and playwrights often bespoke of the romantic purity of dying young, if only fulfilled by love. Growing old, in the poet's eyes, was the agony.[13] Some of this thinking still prevails despite the marked decrease in tubercular deaths in the young. I have known a number of young people dying from cancer in their twenties and thirties who, though frightened at times, have been able to feel uncheated and appropriate. They lived actively in their dying time, not deluded into believing that a cure was imminent, but alive to the potential of their remaining days. A young female friend, aged 35 years, recently expired, five months after the diagnosis of extensive abdominal cancer was made. Most of those months were spent at home with her husband and three children, and together, they shared many tears of sadness and grief.

But that time was precious time to live and to prepare her family for life without her. At one moment during those months she told me that she was really "happy" in a way that she had never been before for now the pretense and argument that had characterized so much of her life could be dropped, and a more peaceful and self-realized person could emerge. Since there was no long future, there was no need to plan to be something that she knew deep inside could never be. In fact, becoming those "things" would have been for appearances for others, not for herself. Irritable marital combativeness disappeared and supporting lovingness emerged. Her one regret was that this self-truth, emerging in this future limited time, could not have been hers, with concommitant loving, long before in her life. With full love of family and in peace with self, she died after several days of coma, after saying peaceful and gratified good-byes to all.

A recent report concerned the dying of a twenty-year-old woman from cancer. She made tape recordings of her last months and is reported to have commented that she was "not afraid of death" at the ripe "old" age of twenty. Her husband concurred that she was in "pretty good spirits all the time" although it was a relief for him that she finally died, for there were some physically rough days near the end. Perhaps the young are fortunate in dying when they do, for idealism, love and purpose remain vital commodities that have not been challenged out of existence by defacing institutions in life.[14]

Fear is frequently a property of the unknown. We are often afraid of what death brings because it is of such an unknown dimension. We do not know what is exchanged for the end of our individual lives as we know them. Be it nothingness, or a vague life form, or resurrection in our present body habitant, it is simply unknown. But added to this dimension of discomfort with death is the fact that our modern society has made dialogues and discussions on death unacceptable.

America, in general, has been accused of being a death-denying society (if America can be classified ever as a single society). In the decades of this century there has appeared to be a dirth of open discussion as to the meaning of death, except of course, in a fundamental religious fashion. But with the watering down of fundamentalistic religion in much of America, usually urban America, death discussion has tended to disappear.

And this general proscription against airing this phenomenal, awesome and eternal human problem has been witnessed not only in social relations, but in the realm of legitimate social science investigation as well. Socially, death and dying are not issues likely to be discussed at an evening's gathering, at a dinner table, at a church luncheon. It may be permissible to mention that so and so died or is quite ill and near death, but such statements, after evincing the usual look and sigh of dismay, are then dismissed and little or no personal interpretation, argument or meaning develops. Few theatrical or Hollywood productions search authentically into the meaning of personal death or suffering from death, although violence, revenge, pursuit, fantasy and heroics abound. Death is delivered for entertainment, not for intimate exploration.

We are less encased in a conspiracy of silence regarding dying and death today, although we are far from liberated. Most people still suffer thoughts privately, or evade thoughts as they must, on the great issues of personal death and personal bereavement. A general social avoidance of discusssing death and its meanings openly helps create difficulty and a lonely anguish for many when dealing with death. In such circumstances, fear, operating in loneliness, can seldom be eased.

While it is true that most people, young and old, do not dwell continuously or even frequently on the subject, confrontations are demanded of us in one way or another. Beyond arbitrary and distant violence, disruptive as that is, each person must face the death of a loved one sooner or later and must arrange, in denial, despair, indifference or joy, his own death at some point. Secrecy in the matter does him a severe injustice and forces him into solitary and lonely contemplation with little opportunity to share his fears and anxieties. Common exposure is no guarantee of peace when contemplating death, but the pressing thoughts of abandonment, darkness, emptiness, annihilation, suffering, pain and meaninglessness need to be explored and worked through if the fears of death during life are to be mitigated, and if man is to feel that he has a right to be in control of his death as well as of his life.

Degeneration of the meaning of death places a great burden on the survivors of a death, accentuating the fear in one's own death. Funeral practices today reflect the loss of communal and ritualistic meaning of the death and tend to emphasize practices that are supposedly helpful for the living via disguise and deception. The growth of the professional secular funeral director has displaced the sacred symbolization ritual of the clergy and has displaced the family intimacy at death.

Not long ago, especially in rural America, it was customary for the women in the family to wash and clothe the body at death and for the men to build the simple pine casket. A simple church and graveside ceremony followed. The modern funeral director did not exist until recently, and certainly the steel and chromium caskets, the embalming, the makeup to look better than life, the elaborate funeral home with the living room decor and atmosphere, all are modern and expensive contrivances. The "sacred city" concept of the community cemetery has been replaced by massive and congested cemeteries at the side of a vigorous superhighway and are uninviting as places for visiting, reflecting and momentary reunion with the dead.

W. Lloyd Warner wrote of the cemetery as a "sacred place, where the gravestones are the hard, enduring signs which anchor man's projection of his innermost fantasies and private fears about the certainty of his own death, the uncertainty of his ultimate future, on an external symbolic object made safe by tradition and the sanction of religion." The modern urban cemetery, distant, impersonal and seldom visited in life, has little role in anchoring man's "private fears." [15]

Modern psychiatry has assured us that one cannot accept the image of one's own death. Our own death is unimaginable. Whenever we attempt to see our personal selves as dead, we are immediately spectators to the image, and therefore one must be alive to see death. The assertion can therefore be made that no one can believe in his own death. In the subconscious, every one of us is supposedly convinced of his own immortality. Perhaps we could not live through our lives without some inner fantasy that regardless of all lessons in life, we are each exempted from the universal demand for a death. Or perhaps it is not a personal death that is not imaginable as a personal annihilation. Perhaps most people want some sense of immortality, if not through personal resurrection, then through seed, good works, history, or even identification with mankind, or nature. As Hamlet says, dying, at the end of the play, "and in this harsh world, draw they breath in pain, to tell my story." [11]

The essential point I think, is that modern man is responsible for the meaning of his individual life, and for those near and dear to him. To confront fears of death is to have an opportunity of growth to new maturity in dealing with those who are now dying, and to prepare for ourselves and for those to whom we are responsible, a better facing of life and death. Since we do not enter into communal patterns of death, we are faced with what we do about our individual deaths. Either we prepare ourselves to be in control of our personal deaths, or we abnegate that control to another who will have us die by someone else's prescriptions. If we are not prepared to think out clearly the personal meaning of our deaths, we become the "victims" of someone else's meaning for our deaths.

If death is nothing but fear, and if fearing prevents us from thinking and acting, we then become less than human. People dying of chronic long-term illness often find themselves caught up in systems of medical care that direct the nature and style of their dying. For many, this may be the only way. Dependent upon others for most decisions in life, that dependency remains into death. But surely these are not absolute conditions and can be examined with the hope of diminishing fear and encouraging strength.

[1]Freud, Sigmund: Beyond the pleasure principle, 1920. In *The Complete Psychological Works of Sigmund Freud,* standard edition, James Strachey, Ed. London, Hogarth Press, 1955, Vol. 18.

[2]Eissler, K.R.: *The Psychiatrist and the Dying Patient.* New York, International Universities Press, 1955.

[3]Rheingold, Joseph C.: *The Mother, Anxiety and Death: The Catastrophic Death Complex.* Boston, Little, Brown, 1967. The author presents a detailed discussion of the fears of the child and the adult, derived from a punitive mother figure.

[4]Bakan, David: *Disease, Pain and Sacrifice: Toward a Psychology of Suffering.* Chicago, The University of Chicago Press, 1968.

[5]Lepp, Ignace: *Death and Its Mysteries.* New York, Macmillan, 1968.

[6]Choron, Jacques: *Death and Modern Man.* New York, Collier, 1964.

[7]Plato: *Apology.* In *The Last Days of Socrates.* Reprint, translated by H. Tredennick. Baltimore, Penguin, 1969.

[8]*Ars Moriendi: The Book of the Craft of Dying,* Francis M.M. Compter, Ed. London, Longmans Green, 1917, Chs. 1, 2.

[9]Taylor, Jeremy: *The Whole Works of the Rt. Rev. Jeremy Taylor,* Reginald Heber, Ed. London, Ogle, Duncan, 1822, Vol. IV.

[10]Montaigne, Michel de: *The Complete Works of Montaigne,* Donald Frame, Ed. Stanford, Calif., Stanford University Press, 1948.

[11]Paz, Octavio: *The Day of the Dead.* In R. Fulton (Ed.): *Death and Identity.* Somerset, N.J., Wiley, 1965.

[12]Erikson, Eric H.: *Identity and the Life Cycle: Psychological Issues.* 1959, Vol. I, No. 1, monograph I.

[13a]Johnston, Ben: *It is Not Growing Like a Tree.* In *L. Perrine* (Ed.): *Sound and Sense.* New York, Harcourt, Brace & World, 1959.

[13b]Housman, A.E.: *To an Athlete Dying Young.* In C. Main and P. Seng (Eds.): *Poems.* Belmont, Calif., Wadsworth, 1961.

[14]Death closes her final chapter, *New York Daily News,* November 7, 1971.

[15]Warner, W. Lloyd: *The City of the Dead.* In R. Fulton (Ed.): *Death and Identity.* Somerset, N.J., Wiley, 1965.

[16]Shakespeare, William: *Hamlet,* George Lyman Kittredge, Ed., Boston, Ginn, 1939.

CHAPTER III

THE INDIGNITIES OF DYING

THE MAJORITY OF Americans today will die of chronic illness in a rather slow, lingering fashion. Acute and unexpected death will continue to occur from heart attacks, accidents and violence. But for most of us, growing older and developing cancer, a failing heart, a failing blood circulatory system in the brain, will be our future. This is not said as a morbidly gratifying prediction, but in the need to examine ourselves as individual humans struggling to make sense of our existence. Although not so apparent when healthy, a major problem for many of us will be how we perceive of ourselves in the biologic suffering that life brings, and in the attitude that we bring to these biologic events. We really have only one of two choices in regard to suffering and dying—either we attempt to find meaning and stay in reasonable control of our destiny as long as conscious intellect remains, or we allow ourselves to be caught up in futility and hopelessness and give ourselves over to someone else for control.

In the practical world of today, a simple statement of an either/or choice of this kind may appear inane at first glance. Since most people do not want to die, nor in fact grow old, nor indeed become chronically ill, we often assume that all of our energies should be linked to finding new medical methods of preventing and curing diseases and keeping aging at a distance. By "we" I am referring to a national public policy or thought. Diseases, as mentioned, are not "good things," and should be eliminated or overcome. But to see disease, or aging, in this light only, and not to address the question of chronic illness and mortality as events inherent in life itself is to play ostrich to some of the most pressing of human issues. On a national scale, there seems to be little effort exerted to help people

[33]

derive both a meaning in their dying, and a manner of maintaining control of the ways of dying.

Chronic illness makes us aware of our mortality. As we look at the meaning of illness in this light, we begin with the facts and fears of death, and we have just examined some of these. If we philosophically, as a society, or in our family circles, or as singular individuals, conceive of death only as fearful, and if our response to that fear is only as flight, then we are paralyzed when a confrontation with death occurs. Accepting an inevitability in death allows us to prepare for growth and meaning even if fear remains.

Perhaps in some ways we must learn from the ancient Persian legend of "Appointment in Samarra." The legend tells of a servant who bursts into his Master's quarters pleading for a fast horse to flee to Samarra because he had just met Death while walking in the marketplace in Bagdad. The Master granted the servant's request, but a bit later while walking in the marketplace, met Death sitting near a tree. "Why did you frighten my servant," inquired the Master? And Death replied, "I did not wish to frighten him. I was just a bit startled to see him here for I had an appointment with him in Samarra later tonight." [1]

Fearful as the confrontation with an abstract concept of death may be for most people, the slow, lingering process of dying of a chronic illness is yet more distressing. For in the process of dying, is the living loss of all those values that make life livable. Americans are brought up to cherish good health, success, cleanliness, independence, sexuality, good looks. There is little *value* seen in suffering and tragedy. They are unwelcomed, and are to be avoided as purposeless and useless dimensions. Dying is the inexorable and visible eradication of culturally stated personal meanings and concepts. We define our self-image, our sense of personal esteem, in relation to the way we see ourselves fulfilling the imperatives of our cultural values. The suffering that emerges in illness is not just physical pain, but is the loss of a good self-image and of the self-esteem that depended on being synchronous or in touch with these expressed cultural values. The dissolution of the body in chronic, wasting disease is the dissolution of those things that make life worthy. With loss of these worthy things, the very meaning to life begins to fade, to be replaced by feelings of agony, anger, futility and helplessness.

A highly cherished ideal, or value, for most of us, is a sense of independence. A fatal illness, with slow dissolution, brings about the gradual loss of independence, with an increasing need to be dependent on others, known and unknown. I am not implying that all people are necessarily independent and that dependency needs are not a characteristic of our lives, but most people feel that they can safely be dependent on only a few trusted individuals in their world. In a society that cherishes the notion of appearing independent, self-reliant and always able, the image of the loss of such characteristics as occurs in the slow process of dying, is a crushing one.

American culture has been described as the worship of the doing. We feel comfortable if we are able to master our immediate environment by doing things or watching things being done. Physical actions are important. Our energies tend to be muscular ones, not contemplative ones. Quiet reflection may be accepted for a vacationing moment or for a scholarly honor, but not as a way of life. Even our intellectuals are exhorted to be in the midst of things of action. The ivory tower as a place of pure thought is snickered at as nonrelevant to life's active pace.

The loss of the potential for doing, the loss of muscular, exertive physical motion is extremely hard to accept. Slow dying broadly carries this implication, an inability to be in control of muscular faculties, a dissolution of the doing body. In this regard, aging and chronic disease are often entwined with the state of dying, for all these conditions carry the implicit message of loss of muscular ability and thus the loss of doing. The loss of being able to do makes someone dependent on another for that doing.

In speaking to patients with chronic and serious illness, I have heard over and over the word "burden." "I do not want to become a burden to my family." The interpretation is given that one has value as a person only when able to do, the doing for others and for self, and that one becomes a burden when one can no longer do. But as a person gets closer to death, especially through a long, lingering illness, there is a marked diminution in doing with a resultant increase in burdening. People are frequently distressed at the burdensomeness and will choose to go into a hospital or nursing home to avoid burdening their families. In so doing, they often resign themselves to death, withdrawing from meaningful interchange with others.

"Burden" means dependence. In such dependence, the attitude of the *others,* those depended on, becomes most important. With the growth of professional responsibility as against kindship responsibility for problem solution, the dependence is not just on family, who may in fact be many miles away, but on institutions, doctors, nurses, technicians, social workers, etc. This becomes a dependence on relative unknowns and uncertainties. It is hard to trust unknown commodities. People are suspicious of the unknown and frequently possess barriers and defenses against letting others come to know them. When such suspicion is fortified by an attitude of not caring to know in the care-givers, the sick are forced to turn inward into their loneliness and fears. Existing problems such as weakness, pain, breathlessness, or nausea become aggravated and exacerbated through fear, uncertainty, distrust and loneliness. If one is uncertain as to who can be depended upon to truly help, an individual becomes even more alone in his suffering.

In dying, not only is muscular doing lost, but so may be the loss of control of one's simple bodily functions such as seeing, feeling, hearing and perhaps even more importantly, urinating and defecating, eating and cleaning. The vision of oneself as a helpless thing, lying in bed, unable to wash, unable to eat by one's own strength, unable to void or to eliminate in privacy, is deeply upsetting to most of us, healthy or sick. Especially painful is the image of oneself put into such a condition, in a strange hospital with strangers attending to these needs. Can an image of incontinence with soiling of sheets, tubes inserted into the urinary bladder to control leakage and perhaps even worse insults, be a part of the definition of dignity or self-worth?

We are horrified to think of ourselves or our loved ones, caught up in such dissolution. We fear an impersonalization, a need to expose all of one's body to any interested, or perhaps just even a curious stranger, such as the young professional, or the young person training to be a professional. If the hospital is hard to take in this regard, the image of one's spouse or children caring for these bodily functions at home may be even more offensive to one's sense of independence and dignity. The smells, odors and sights of sickness are repugnant for the sick as well as the healthy. Yet most people have seen loved ones in just this state, lying in bed with complete loss of self-control, frozen into dependency, as the disintegration goes on due to a long-standing illness. How frightening to think about our own dying when this is the vision we have. How necessary to run when we are confronted with such dissolution.

While the problem is not simply modern medical practices, it does seem that medicine and hospitals today bear some responsibility for prolonging life that is no longer worthy life. Burden is shame and humiliation in our minds and bitterness in our hearts. That a physician and a nurse will continue to keep one alive in this state after months of painful dissolution, often seems less than honorable. It is painful to witness these physiologic failings in a loved one, and shattering to imagine ourselves the same way, while our loved ones watch and are uncomfortable, sharing our decline with us.

Some of this anxiety for being a burden comes both from a true concern for another's pleasure, and a fear that if we burden another person, it is an indication that we are less than good and therefore, not very lovable. And we worry that if we are a burden to another, perhaps they will abandon us when we most need them.

A young patient of mine with widespread cancer, developed severe pain on the day of a New Year's evening. Married, she was alone in her apartment and was forced to call her brother and sister-in-law as well as her home physician for help and comfort. Despite medication, her pain lingered and the couple spent the evening with her. For days afterward, this sick young lady repeatedly echoed that she was becoming increasingly burdensome, and hoped she would soon die. How terrible it was for her to spoil her brother's New Year's Eve plans. She just could not keep doing that. Not only was she concerned for her family's well-being, and not only did she question her right to use her relations as she did, but she was afraid that they would think badly of her.

Perhaps there was a time when family and community was less concerned with the concept of burden. Perhaps sons, daughters, husbands, wives, mothers, fathers, friends and neighbors accepted interaction in the human condition as expected and natural, and caring for a loved one was neither an option nor a struggle, either for the care-givers or the care-receivers. Since life was not extended by tubes and instruments, people lived with less continued disintegration visible. Without so many hospitals and nursing homes and so many professionals, the giving and receiving of care was probably a natural order of things, and burden, as a concept, had less impact.

Chronic diseases are not always imminently fatal. Disorders such as diabetes or thyroid insufficiency may be chronic in the sense that a person may live with the problem for many, many years, but nevertheless may live quite, or nearly, normally. But such illnesses as kidney diseases, pulmonary emphysema, cancer and the like, are not only chronic, they are frequently fatal. Many of these illnesses command much medical attention. These illnesses are a threat to a person's narcissistic self-image. A person's concept of his self-worth is often invested in a particular body part or style of living, and the way a person sees and interprets a particular organ or body part plays enormously on his sense of integrity, self-worth and his perceived ability to be liked and loved. A fatal illness such as cancer frequently results in disfiguring surgical procedures, such as bowel resection, with a subsequent colostomy altering the flow of fecal material, or a breast amputation. Even if these procedures result in the cure from illness, much psychologic damage can ensue requiring considerable attention, if self-esteem is to be restored.

For the actual patient who is not cured but only temporarily benefitted, this surgical alteration can be the first of a series of assaults that increasingly threaten the sense of attraction, livingness and worthiness. A woman who has invested, psychologically, great importance in her appearance, and especially in the existence of her breasts, may be not only deeply wounded by surgery such as a mastectomy, but may begin an unconscious thought process of giving up, defining herself now as being unloveable, and becoming resigned that death may be better than life. This feeling of worthlessness can be easily enforced by husband, by sisters and by unthinking friends as they go about their daily lives failing to recognize or understand the psychological wound.

As an illness worsens, and the involved person gets sicker, more medical procedures are needed, while fewer and fewer of the usual pleasures in life are available. More and more constraints upon daily options in life develop. The meaning and pleasure of food changes, the pleasures of deciding the where and the when to go diminish, the ability to enjoy the outdoors decreases, the sensual pleasures of seeing and touching recedes. More and more time is spent in hospitals or nursing homes. It is not hard to imagine how frustrating, how hurting and how diminished a once-healthy individual can feel. As a person is dying, (and by dying I mean that period of time when a slow but undeniable weakening of strength towards death proceeds, a period that can last not only for days but for weeks and months), there may be a continual wound to one's self-image, self-value and self-esteem, to the self-centered meaning of a life.

Instead of finding ways of shoring up that esteem, those people in the environment of a patient—family, friends and professionals—often innocently aid in the erosion. For example, seldom recognized is the importance for a declining individual to be supported in doing something like getting down a flight of stairs to make a visit to the doctor or to an important family member. Concerned family members might well try to persuade the sick individual to rest and wait until he recovers enough strength for the visit. Such dissuasion, often well-meaning, detracts enormously from the few options left to the individual, with consequent further decrease in self-value.

There are other dominant cultural values that put the sick and the dying into an unattractive position. Already alluded to is the value of individualism as opposed to linearity or collaterality. All men live in social relations of one kind or another. The insistence of individuality, with its rights and privileges, can also bring a self-accusation for failure, with heightened loneliness, in the face of personal disaster. If the joys of success are accentuated in individualism, ("every boy, or perhaps girl, can become president"), the impact of failure is also individualistic. Health today is being stressed as a personal responsibility. We are told that the food we eat, the rest we get, the exercises we do are our personal responsibility. We are told to live right and to live young. We are warned to watch our intake of animal fat, of cholesterol, of starches, of proteins, of vitamins. Smoking causes thus and so, alcohol punishes us thus and so, drugs destroy us in this way. We are warned to jog, to run, to walk, to bicycle. Health and vigor are to be protected by our doing for our-

selves. And, if you notice anything amiss, see the doctor immediately. The American Cancer Society preaches the early warning signs and urges no delay.

Obviously, a healthy populace has important meaning for a nation, and individuals should bear some personal responsibility for their nonhealth. But sufficient knowledge of the causal factors in most, if not all, chronic disease, is far from known, and what constitutes the characteristics of early and therefore curable disease, is far from defined. However, as responsibility is placed on the individual for his own health, illness has the overtones of a personal failure, rather than as a necessary dimension of life. Dying then becomes the ultimate failure. It is a bit unfair to stress personal responsibility until there is little doubt that personal responsibilty is that critical to health. For example, women are told to self-examine their breasts for early detection of lumps—they are urged to see their physicians immediately. But there is little evidence to date that the woman who "feels" that lump and runs immediately to her physician, will be guaranteed a cure if the lump is cancer. The ultimate outcome of the disease is frequently unrelated to this finding, for the disease may already be considerably advanced by the time the lump is discernable. I do not wish to imply fatalism, nor that women should not see their physicians when they find a lump, nor to imply that women should not feel for lumps. But women with breast cancer must be helped to understand that their very lives do not depend on their own hands finding a lump. Their hands are not always able to detect small, very early cancers. The burden for their lives did not rest on their failing to find the lump earlier. The way that the message is now delivered implies strongly that a personal responsibility for one's cancer exists in one's own hands.

In addition to the dissolution of one's body, the loss of control of one's doing, the diminution of feelings of adequacy and self-esteem and the potential of self-blame, the dying individual must often confront the fact that he is giving up those things that he knows and loves about life. A slow dying moves to deprive us gradually of all we love of this good life on earth, and how hard it is to confront this giving up. In people, in things, in places, in work—in these and more are we invested, in all that is the secular.

And since we are so unsure of what death brings, how impossible it is to think about giving up all that we know and will never experience in any way again.[2] "Dying wouldn't be so bad if I could be sure that there was sex after death." For many, to die slowly is to mourn the loss of these lovely objects in life, and such mourning is sad and depressing. Further, dying forces us to confront our life's indecisions, uncertainties, ambiguities, errors and failures. It is hard to die by degrees, having so much yet to be done, so many acts of contrition to attend, so much forgiveness to work through, so much vanity to exercise.

Most people organize their lives toward the future and invest that future with chores, plans, jobs, expectations and hopes. Much of what we think we would like to do, to be, to become, is left to some uncertain future date. It is somewhere in the indeterminate future that certain life issues will be resolved. An awareness of dying forces us to confront the fact that many of these dreams and plans will now go unfinished. It is painful to confront these issues. A sense of insufficiency, or inadequacy, can easily overwhelm the sick individual, deepening an already existing sense of despair.

Persons dying of a chronic illness become particularly vulnerable, especially as death draws close, not only to biologic disruption with problems of pain, incontinence, breathlessness, etc., but to the pains of the loss of meaningful interpretations of life and to feelings of depression, self-blame, worthlessness and lovelessness. When such losses of self-image occur and feelings of burdensomeness and dependency deepen, a person's stature is cripplingly diminished in his eyes.

Our values and behavior in American (if not Western) culture, tend to have the healthy and the well share in this interpretation of a dying person's worth. As a society, we seem ill-prepared to help the dying maintain a sense of worthiness and esteem. Our educational system from childhood onward, provides little opportunity for people to learn the meaning of sickness, of dignity, or of worthlessness. As a society, we pay little attention to an education as to how to live with, or how to help, those with disability, or how to prepare ourselves, or how to prepare our loved ones, to live while dying. The healthy thus find themselves ill-prepared to face the dying of a loved one, and in our embarrassment and unpreparedness, tend to shy away from meaningful interaction and support.

A dying person, in turn, feeling less sure of himself, less admirable, and less acceptable as a person, depressed by what he is losing in dying, may well appear to be withdrawing from communication with his family and friends. Or he may, in that sense of depression, become demanding, accusative, demeaning, debasing, begging. If allowed, he may even admit to a severe jealousy of those who are well and have a future of vigorus life while he faces nothing but further dissolution. Every shred of his previously controlled, respectful behavior towards others may disappear.

When this happens, people in the immediate environment have a tendency to withdraw even further, thereby fulfilling the self-interpretation of worthlessness. Indeed, it is not difficult to understand such withdrawal, for it is hard to come back for more when a person is destructive in his interpersonal relations. It is a commonplace observation that as illness progresses and death approaches, friends and family do recede. The patient's expectation of isolation becomes a reality and the loneliness of one's dying is reinforced by the absence of responding, communicating, living presences. Even if loving people do not physically abandon a loved dying one, there is frequently intense embarrassment as to what to say and how to talk to a person with little future, reinforcing the already existing sense of worthlessness and loneliness. The healthy, made uncomfortable by the presence of altered bodies, of weakened faces, of sick countenances, of smells and sights of dying, often wish to be away and not reminded of the frailty of the human potential. In this way, loved people may die in a social and needed sense, long before they are biologically ready for death. Abandonment and withdrawal are all too frequently real.

For the healthy, young, middle-aged or older, much of the fear and pain that exists in their images of what dying means, relates to what has been seen and rehearsed in the dying of a loved one. No man born has not known death. The manner of dying of loved ones, of friends, of associates, tends to create an expectancy for our own dying. The multiple agonies associated with fatal illness and dying today are probably reflected in the oft-recurring answer I have received to the question of choosing a way of dying. Having asked this question to many college and health professional students, and to people in their thirties through sixties, almost invariably the response has been "suddenly and unexpectedly". A quick heart attack is the preferred manner. To face dissolution, disappointment, weakening, dependency, burdensomeness, disfigurement and loss of control is hardly desirable. But unfortunately, a quick and unexpected death is not the lot of most of us.

The initial statement regarding control of our dying thus becomes quite relevant. Since there are so many fears, questions, sorrows and regrets involved in dying, and since what we have witnessed or imagined, in the dying of others has often been so destructive, painful and lonely, in what manner can we talk about control, as if this is a conscious, intelligent process? How can one talk of control if our self-image in dying is so diminished, and the self-esteem necessary to exert control has been imperiled? We will examine these propositions in depth, starting with a control problem faced by the very elderly.

Many elderly face the problem of being forced to live by decisions not theirs but their caretakers. Americans place great value on life for life's sake, not for living's sake. The very elderly, who often have lost all possible joys of life through blindness, deafness, paralysis, senility, inability to communicate, crippling bed-riddenness and loneliness, are frequently kept alive by forced feeding, antibiotics, medical resuscitation and the like in nursing homes, old age homes and hospitals, long after they have made it clear that death would be preferable. A recent letter from an elderly gentleman pleaded for a change in attitudes so that his 93-year old wife might be allowed to simply die. Maimed by a head injury some three years prior, she has become a burden to herself, and residing in a nursing home, was trying to resist eating. However, the nurses were force-feeding her by prying open her mouth with a spoon. The correspondent attempted to persuade the Directress of the nursing home to allow his wife to die if she wished, but was told that the rule was to keep everyone alive as long as possible. The letter was an appeal against forcing the aged to live just to be alive, but as yet there seems to be great difficulty in allowing the powerless to terminate life when the controllers feel the urgency to maintain it.[3]

Many of the elderly find themselves caught in such a vise, forced to stay alive by a caretaking system that has the tools to maintain life at any cost, even against the living's wishes. Some of our best medical agents can often be abused this way. Pneumonia used to be called the "old man's friend." It is so easy to cure a pneumonia now with antibiotics, that the drugs are given even to the sick and weary elderly to cure his one-time friend, forcing life to go on, unrequested and often undesired.

To be in control of one's life and death thus implies having power— the power to prevent unwanted actions of others. This power can be legal, but it also can be moral. The absence of a public policy of discussion and confrontation frequently places the elderly, the weak, the infirm and the dying in a powerless position. Such helplessness is the antagonist of dignity.

[1]Maugham, W. Somerset: *Shippey.* In *The Collected Plays of W. Somerset Maugham.* London, W. Heinemann, 1961, Vol. III, p. 298.

[2]Aldrich, C. Knight: The dying patient's grief. *Journal of the American Medical Association, 184*:329-331, 1963.

[3]Morgan, Arthur E.: A letter printed in the *Washington Post,* January 1, 1972, originally published in the December, of the *Hastings Center Report,* New York.

CHAPTER IV

FATAL ILLNESS AND THE PHYSICIAN

THE EXPLICIT AIM of modern medicine is the cure of illness in general, and certainly the elimination of fatal illness. This is not only a primary aim, but almost an exclusive one. The modern hospital has become an efficiency plant continually being refurbished with the latest equipment directed at curing and correcting ills. Doctors are constantly encouraged to continue their learning in regard to the latest definitions and knowledge of disease, and to newly developing ways of applying modern treatments. The federal government allocates considerable resources, small though they may be compared to the national defense budget, to the basic sciences which hold as their eventual objective, the elucidation of the properties of cells and organs so that this information can be applied to the elimination of human disease processes. These efforts certainly reflect society's interests. Anybody who has suffered the loss of a family member from a fatal illness such as cancer, cannot doubt that this fearful and dreadful disease should be eradicated. In fact, the argument is often heard that what we need is more money in this direction, and if only a portion of the treasury spent on the war effort could be reallocated to medical biology, research and experimental treatment, diseases such as cancer would be quickly eliminated, to the gratification of the entire world. The present presidential campaign to launch a Conquest-of-Cancer drive, with the President as commander-in-chief of the campaign, finds universal favor despite some dissension as to how best to get the job done. With this crusade launched against cancer, heart disease will most likely be next, what with diseases of the heart and blood vessels being the primary killer in America.

Although cancer and heart disease are found in all age groups with the young and middle-aged not being completely spared, these diseases are found principally at the further reaches of the life scale, in people in their sixties and seventies and eighties. Since men do not die just of their natural lives but of their illnesses, especially those associated with growing older, the aging process itself becomes entwined with these mentioned physical disturbances. Energies are now being concentrated on research into aging so that eventually either a postponement of the aging processes as we know them, or their eventual elimination, will occur. With this elimination, a parri-passu absence of serious, chronic illness is expected to follow. In this manner, aging by itself can now be classified as a fatal illness. In our youth-oriented culture, aging is already considered a calamity, and the insult of being elderly, already felt by many aged people, is aggravated by the research objective of wiping out aging entirely. The elimination of the aging process has always caught the imagination of men and historically, through search or bargain, men have attempted to secure extended youth. Wandering in out-of-the-way geographies for various elixirs has been the lot of more than the occasional age-fearing explorer. The bartering of one's soul to the devil for youth and vitality is a recurrent fantasy theme in literature, although there is usually a devastating denouement when the devil eventually comes to claim his due.

This emphasis on aging, as if it were something of a wrong or an illness, or a time of life when such things as chronic diseases occur, is emphatically reinforced by our demand for youthfulness. The elderly not only have little to contribute in this technologic society, but they are now accused of eating into the national budget by their requirements for health and medical care, special housing, special nursing homes and the like. They are not treated as a group deserving of a special funding in dedication to their efforts, their accomplishments and their value as citizens. Condemnation of the elder as an accumulation of faults and purposelessness is poor support for their self-esteem, and a frightening prophecy for all who must one day assume the role and position of an elder.

If aging is seen as a time of degeneration, uselessness, waste and illness, then the elimination of the aging process seems justified as a major national goal. But just what does such a goal entail? An effective elimination of the aging process is truly tantamount to eradicating natural mortality, for the many disorders associated with growing older would expectedly be eliminated as well. Is such ending of death to be desired? From what we know of checks and balances, the ending of death requires the simultaneous ending of reproduction and new birth. As mortality rates around the world have been dramatically dropping in this century, population explosions are already threatening the physical, ecologic and economic viability of nations and mankind in general. The control of birth rates has become a major problem for civilization today. The elimination of death is the ending of birth, with biologic, social and individual stagnation. For surely the intensity of life and its joys are entwined with the intimation of impermanence, of mortality. One can live fully and deeply because the secret is propelling. Nothing is forever.

If the goal is not immortality but simply extension of life, then we still face a period of aging, if not when we are sixty, then when we are one hundred and sixty. Unless the concept would be that no one need grow old but that at some controllable moment in a vigorous and healthy life, say at age one hundred (or some other arbitrary figure), one would just die or be killed. Is it possible to imagine that a man would give up this world voluntarily when in the possession of youth and vigor simply because a time had arbitrarily come? Can men live by such a design? An extension of life in which aging is not eliminated but merely postponed would present us with the same set of physical and psychological problems as today, as people would come to expect that one hundred sixty years was the norm of anticipated survival time. But our societal, economic and political problems might well be fantastic. Birth control would be even more critical than now, and population masses could become still more difficult to control. Jobs, retirement, purpose, schooling, all would need total retooling. It is not that the required remaking of life activities could not be accomplished, it is simply that we do not seem to be paying corollary attention to what extended life time would demand.

The attention of the medical educational format has been the control and eradication of the major killing disorders such as cancer and heart disease. Young students in medicine, nursing and allied fields are taught ways of helping people to get better, and the student comes to invest himself in the idea that the caretaking of people means getting them better. The young physician is taught that the combat against illnesses, fatal and otherwise, is the primary concern and demand of his profession. He is also taught that medicine is science, and that to know and understand the basic physiologic and chemical events in health and disease is imperative. As massive data accumulates as to the mechanisms implicit in illness, and larger and broader grants of money are launched to expand bodies of data, the young physician finds that most of his time is spent in sorting out and mastering this knowledge. The young medical student and the young physician-in-training also quickly learn that the rewards within the hierarchal systems in medicine, especially academic medicine, are given to scientifically oriented thinking and acting, and not towards humanistic growth and development. Medical schools seem oriented toward accepting students with a "scientific" bent rather than a human caretaking bent.

Specialization within the medical profession has developed in response to the continued growth of knowledge, with the recognition that few men can deal with all the complicated material gathered and being gathered, relative to disease and biology. The accent on specialization narrows the dimensions of any one particular physician's medical horizons, and results in fewer and fewer generalists and more and more specialists. The average citizen now requires a coterie of doctors to attend to his routine needs, such as an internist for himself; an obstetrician for the arrival of his children; a gynecologist (who may well not be the same person as the obstetrician) for feminine advice; a pediatrician for the newborn and growing ones; a surgeon (or surgeons) for hernias, gall bladders and appendices; an ophthalmologist for eyes; an otolaryngologist for ears; and of course, a psychiatrist for that personal discomfort with the living world. Now a scientific basis for medicine and resultant specialization is the beneficial fruit of elaborating knowledge and certainly offers to the sick individual an opportunity for resolution of his health problems such as never before existed.

But the growth of specialties in medical care has meant the abandonment of two previously desired principals, namely that a physician should know his patient and family well, and that he should be present to care for one and attend the others in an accustomed setting of home or in a community-based office. Specialists depend not just on factual data for their care-giving, but also on special equipment (such as X-rays and blood analyzing apparatus) that allows for more complete exploration of the body and its internal contents. Such equipment is expensive, nonportable and frequently to be found only in or near hospitals. Physicians have retreated from homes and community-based offices to deliver vastly better investigation and advice in hospitals or in offices at or near the hospitals.

Many other reasons, social, intellectual and family, have helped in this retrenchment as to where the physician gives his care, but specialization certainly has been a major determinant. Fewer and fewer physicians are available to live in communities and practice there. More and more become full-time or part-time hospital employees with offices nearby. The modern physician need not live in the neighborhood of his hospital, especially if the institution is in a large, urban setting, and certainly need not participate in the life of that neighborhood. The decrease of the community-based physician has resulted in burgeoning services in the accident or emergency rooms of hospitals, as the latter grow toward becoming the primary giver of medical care. There is little "personal" in the accident room.

The appeal of the laboratory as the avenue of knowledge and development has been greatly enhanced by funding from federal agencies and by large private foundations. In addition, a sizeable clinical trial program has also been with us lately in which experimental drugs or procedures are administered to patients, for the sake of improving applied treatments. These trials are often based on a modicum of information as to the mechanisms of how and why the many new experimental drugs work. Although human trials are always preceded by careful laboratory and animal experiments, many of the physiological or pharmacological factors changed or influenced by the action of the experimental drug cannot be fully understood without human trial, and frequently, not even then. The search is for more effective drugs to combat disease prospers in a more or less fortuitous manner, and with the hope that an "effective" agent will be uncovered.

This clinical investigative approach has been applied in the treatment of several fatal illnesses, of which cancer probably has seen the largest financial investment. Many new drugs, (after extensive laboratory research and animal experimentation) have been made available to the clinical cancer specialists. The federal government, through the National Cancer Institute, has screened thousands and thousands of compounds in the past twenty years, either in its own laboratories or through contracts made with various drug firms or other agencies. Hundreds of these drugs have been released for clinical trials and thousands and thousands of cancer patients have been given these agents.

A few of the drugs have been successful in changing the course of the disease in a small number of patients. Such illnesses as childhood leukemia, Hodgkins Disease, Wilms tumor of the kidney in childhood and lymphomatous diseases in general, have been extraordinarily changed by the presence of these drugs. Some women with advanced breast cancer have been helped as has an occasional sufferer from many other types of cancer. New experimental drugs or combinations of drugs may well continue to improve the problems of the cancer patient in the future. The significance of the gains made with these drugs and with newer approaches in immunology, offer seductive appeal, so that each and every patient with advanced cancer has the right, or perhaps obligation, to receive these agents. Even if the patient is not immediately benefitted, someone else with the disease in the future might be.

Most of the experimental drugs on trial today are potent, not just against the cancer cell, but against many other cells and organs in the body. Thus toxic side effects are frequent, ranging from the occasional drug-induced death of the patient, to more frequent nausea, vomiting, diarrhea, hair-loss, skin rashes and so on. The cells of the blood, white cells and platelets especially, are frequently injured, resulting in the lowering of their numbers in the blood stream with ensuing infections and bleeding episodes. Depending on the drug used, other side effects on normal tissues may be seen. Sometimes these effects are rather mild and sometimes quite delibrating. The goal of the cancer physician, of course, is to halt the growth of cancer or eliminate the cancer cells if he can, and not to cause the patient discomfort from the treatment. But if side effects are necessary with today's drugs, they will have to be tolerated. Patients are not actually forced to take these drugs and it is conceivable that they can always refuse the drug once informed of the potential toxic effects.

With these great and continuing efforts against cancer, the patient is frequently under active treatment until he dies. He ends his days, either because the disease was too advanced and he could not be helped, or because his disease became resistant to the treatments, or because he failed to respond to medicine's ministrations. Since the objective is cure or prolongation of life, efforts are directed against death. (But this is not the case for all people. In certain hospitals a frequent alternative is to discharge the terminal patient and send him elsewhere to die, such as a nursing home or extended care facility. This decision is frequently made in the larger civic and teaching hospitals where beds are valued for curable and/or teaching problems).

The extent to which efforts against death are directed can sometimes appear bizarre. A California physician called me recently concerning his mother in Boston. In her seventies, she did not have cancer, but had suffered a stroke and had been in coma, totally unresponsive, for the preceding five months. Her biologic life was being maintained by a feeding tube passed into the stomach via her nose and by intravenous fluids. She was in a small hospital in Boston at a cost of $140 per day of which Medicare paid the majority, but the family had to assume $50 daily. The family was eager to have it over with and could see no sense in continuing life. The physician in charge just could not discontinue the maintenance treatments. He was quite amenable to the family's changing physicians or institutions, but the son could not find a practicing physician who would consent to take the case. And so a completely comatose, elderly woman was being kept alive. Of an even greater irony was the fact that this woman had told her family, some months prior to this stroke, that she was quite ready to die and that she hoped no one would force her to stay alive when her "time came."

In general, men die as the victims of disease. They die when the medical profession runs out of resources to treat their disorders or when the patient fails to respond to ongoing treatment. The notion that men should die and can be helped to die well is virtually foreign to the educational and operational designs of medical thinking. It may well be that such concept is also foreign to many men dying. For if a person has a fatal illness that is under attack from all possible corners of the nation's health and research resources, then that person has the right to demand especial attention to his illness. An unnecessary death is absurd and should not be countenanced. Few people, except perhaps the very elderly, consciously welcome death.

Our health care systems in general are not geared for dying from fatal illness. For many kinds of health problems, an economic medical care design in which specialization and efficiency dominate, is necessary and just. A large amount of unnecessary injury, maiming, suffering and death still exists in this country because effective and economical medical care is not available to all, especially in areas where the poor, the disadvantaged, the politically abused, the non-English speaking minorities reside. Specially trained professionals may be less needed than good generalists in such areas until the level of health care can be elevated to some base line from which further improvement would only occur through the presence of highly trained specialists.

For middle class America, urban and suburban based, care by specialists is taken for granted. Given the option of choice, a middle-class broken leg will have a better chance for good union, repair and return to function under the care of an orthopedist. Surgery for a ruptured appendix results in fewer complications and faster recovery in the hands of a well-qualified surgeon in a modern hospital; rare and unusual diseases are better studied and handled in a special unit of a large urban hospital.

But fatal illness requires a whole other dimension, and it is in this realm of diseases associated with pain, suffering and dying that a conflict emerges with the specialized, efficient and economic modern health-care model. Diseases associated with dying are total human illnesses, involving every segment of person, of family, and of community, and require a different medical arrangement. Fatal illness is frequently complicated, requiring the services of many different medical specialists as time proceeds. Most treatments tend to be elaborate, requiring extensive hospitalization time. Caretaking is expensive and many families are rendered economically destitute by the time death occurs. But perhaps of greatest importance, a fatal illness forces a person to focus on the very meaning of his life and on the lives of persons he loves or feels responsible for. A fatal illness forces the person to become more and more dependent on others in his world as time goes on, and gives him fewer and fewer opportunities to exert control of himself. Within a world becoming more and more limited as sickness progresses a fatal illness forces a person to confront the "wrapping up" of his life, to find something of meaning in the life now in the past.

Cancer is an excellent example of these dimensions. The illness begins by a discovery or an uncovering, and a train of medical events then ensues. A set of symptoms or complaints become apparent, acutely or gradually, and a person seeks help from a personal or a clinical physician, usually an internist. The patient is then likely to be referred to another specialist, usually a surgeon. If the person is fortunate, and this is more likely to be so in smaller communities than in large, urban centers, the two specialists will be close friends or associates, and the first physician will be in close contact not only with the second, but with the patient and family as well. If things do not go immediately well, or worsen at a later date, a third specialist may be necessary, frequently in another facility or hospital, depending on the seriousness of the illness and in what area of treatment the problem now falls. With each successive movement to another specialist, the chance of continued close rapport with the first physician diminishes. Each transition may well be discontinuous, requiring new relationships to be established.

This discontinuous special care-giving is especially common in the large city or federal hospitals as well as in the teaching hospitals. But with transitions, something gets lost, namely a closeness and dependency on a stable, continuous, medical figure. The discontinuous system works well to assure that good specialized professional talent is applied to the treatment of the disease, but the price for this conveyor belt can easily be an impersonalization and dehumanization of the individual suffering from the illness. The treating physician and facility frequently expect to follow and care for the individual patient for only a short block of time, and the building of strong, personal relationships is both too time consuming and too unrelated to the defined problem. As referrals to other physicians proceed, the patient and his family learn that there are few indeed who truly care for him as a suffering individual, and find themselves delivering his disease process to various practitioners for their particular skills.

People with cancer have frequently been healthy before developing the symptoms of their illness, and in seeking out a physician, are often making an initial contact. This need to find a physician for the first time is especially true for urban dwellers, and especially for poor urbanites whose social contacts with physicians may have been few, and for the adults in the small nuclear family who have had no personal prior reasons to see a physician. Or they may be relative newcomers to the urban area. Once found, the physician of course, will exert his skills to diagnose the symptoms and signs of the disorder and the surgeon, to whom the patient next turns, does his best, as will the other specialists. Through this array of experts, there is infrequently a close advocate who will guide the individual faithfully and trustingly through these various specialists and remain in close contact at all times. Each discontinuous step requires new relationships to be built and for new faith to be expressed by both parties, the treated and the treating. Physicians with specialties tend to be both highly scientifically oriented and overworked. They are usually just too busy to stay in continuous touch with a patient with a long-term illness who is going from treatment to treatment. Only if a person has a deeply interested private physician, and this is more usual in a smaller community, or if a long-standing social or caretaking bond has existed, will the patient find a personal continuity and ongoing trust.

As new knowledge develops in cancer (as it certainly will) and newer experimental procedures are conceived (as they assuredly will be), discontinuity of care with special treatment will become even more apparent and the loneliness of the patient in transit, more disturbing.

Throughout these multiple attacks on his medical disease, the person is defining his life in the context of his illness. Cancer is a frightening illness; and for many, cancer is more. Many individuals feel a shame in having cancer, others see the illness as retribution for some sin or evil committed or inspired. Some people wish to blame others for making them ill, others wonder why God has singled them out. Most recognize the fatalness in their illness, although there are many who can proudly speak of being cured.

Because of the many and extensive medical procedures that people often go through, they see their bodily images altered and often feel depressed and less than normal. Their sense of self-worth is considerably decreased. Some see their cancers "eating them up," others feel themselves dirty, some fear that they smell badly. All of these assaults and interpretations cause depressions, withdrawal from social involvement, a resignation of worthlessness and lovelessness. Such patients find little pleasure in life, and life holds little positive meaning for them.

Patients as these need a trusting environment with warm personal relations in order to feel at all safe. An ever-changing medical milieu concentrating principally on technologic care, forces patients to bear their real suffering, the suffering of their personal human lives and its meaning, by themselves. In this suffering, tempered by occasional remissions and improvements, the uncured cancer patient moves towards his death.

Taking care of dying patients who do not respond to treatments is a generally unrewarding task. The physician is often a professional whose chief reward comes from getting a sick person well again. Not only does he experience a deep personal gratification in healing, he also feels that he has earned the patient's or the family's gratitude. Committed to scientific understanding and untutored in the arts of consolation, death is a defeat, and the nonresponding or poorly responding patient is a deeply ungratifying experience to deal with. When a specialist's expertise comes to naught for a particular patient, there is a general reluctance to continue on with that individual, especially if the physician feels that there is nothing more that he can do.

If the particular disease processes were consistently curable by these particular medical approaches, specialization and discontinuity would be enough. Medical care-giving need not be directed at changing the total or the long-standing life style of people, and need not be concerned with helping a person find meaning in his life. Religion, philosophy, politics, psychology, sociology are more concerned with these life issues. Routinely, this position seems to me to be eminently justified. It is when a particular disease or illness causes whole life-style changes that attention must be paid to these phenomena as being part of the disease process itself. This truly is the meaning of illness, in which the disturbance is seen from the person's viewpoint and not just from the biological. Needless to say, psychological problems arise in the cure and management of many human physical afflictions, such as the amputation of a leg or the alteration in living habits for the juvenile diabetic. These problems present essential needs for human services beyond the simple disease state.

The problem of a fatal illness is precisely the human perception of dying. The essential conflict for medicine and for people at large resides between an acceptance of dying and death as a basic tribulation of the human condition, and the definition of death as an unacceptable defeat that must always be warred against. An acceptance of death allows us to observe the dying process as a human event, and to dedicate our efforts to helping and improving the living time for a person dying and for his family. The position of death as an unreneging enemy forces us to the position of fighting to the last moment against the vile conqueror, and in fact, denying the need to search for meaning. Perhaps we need not insist on an either-or debate, and perhaps medicine and society can help the dying work through his search for meaning to his illness and his dying, in order to find peace, while at the same time battling against death. But if this is so, then we must pay attention to these human needs.

There are many people who die without accepting their fates, denying their awareness of imminent death and insisting that they are getting better even when all evidence points towards the opposite. Some cling to every opportunity for a few more minutes of life. Most of these latter people are in terrible fright or fear, claiming that they just do not want to or simply cannot. There frequently is nothing positive for which they rage and fight—it is usually a negative thing that fear so easily portrays. There are also those who refuse to accept an imminent death because there is a positive reason to stay alive somewhat longer; some cause, some need, some ideal continues to drive them, continues to need them. These latter individuals do rage and do battle, and all battle is due them, for acceptance of their deaths is merely temporized, not denied or refused. Many people I have known have moved toward an understanding and an acceptance of their dying that does not come out of fear, but has gone beyond fear. There is a sense of wrapping things up, putting things in order, accepting a meaning, a purpose, to their lives. Age has little to do with such acceptance. Children, young adults and the elderly, all have the potential for an acceptance of the end of life. I do not mean that they have given up their lives easily, but that after a long battle with illness and treatments, they have moved psychologically to a reasonable peaceful ending.

Modern medicine does not appear to be tailored toward understanding a particular patient's view or feeling about his illness, nor especially geared toward helping to find acceptance in death. More times than not, some new treatment or other is applied so that no stone is left unturned. Laudable as that latter intention might abstractly be, the individual patient, moving toward an acceptance of death is implored overtly or implicitly, to keep fighting. It is hard to find a peaceful ending in such a therapeutic atmosphere.

In addition, our professional institutions (often by their very existence and function), unwittingly enforce another type of despair. A person's identity and sense of person are expressed in things such as home and possessions, and the control that he has over his body and over events in his environment. Even a small furnished room may become the symbol of one's self. A few personal belongings come to represent security in the present through the past. To be forced to leave home and go into an institution is difficult for a short period, and may be overwhelming when a prolonged period of time is involved. Hospitals are not geared to create a homelike atmosphere even though many newer and more expensive institutions are geared for hotel-like comfort.

Not only are our hospitals and other health institutions frequently not constructed towards homelike existence for the long-term ill, they are especially not geared to enhance human self-esteem needs. Most hospitals are places of efficiency in disease control and are furnished and designed for rapid patient turnover and efficient medical nursing staff performance. The sick role, for a short-term illness, implies giving oneself over to the experts for their studies, testings and treatments. There is a tacit understanding that the patient will give up control of himself and allow others to become privy to secret body parts and with caution, to some secret thoughts. The aim of this exercise in the sick role is restitution to health, and a short hospital stay is allowable. When a convalescent period is indicated, home is where we go and gradually more and more self-control is regained. Still, even when a short period of time is involved, many greatly resent the indignities found in the hospital. Hospital customs such as johnnies that do not fit; tests scheduled to begin at seven in the morning; removal of large quantities of blood without prior warning or instruction; interns, residents, medical students, barging in without asking permission; these, plus other types of similar behavior, irk us because they reflect that personal concern is replaced by organizational efficiency.

When the sick role is not short-lived but protracted and exhausting, and the hospital stay prolonged, the importance of self to the workings of the institution diminishes further. There is often a feeling of irritation and exasperation on the part of the nursing and medical staff as improvement does not happen. Recurrent hospitalizations for treatments that may work but for only short blocks of time, gradually produce the same irritating feelings of helplessness and ineptitude on the parts of medical and nursing staffs as well as families and patients. A gradual weariness with the situation develops. As the patient is dying, these feelings of ineptitude, unrewardedness and irritation in the medical staff frequently lead to a withdrawal of interest and of contact; staff time becomes less and less available; nurses take a longer time to answer buzzers; doctors are busy elsewhere.

During this time in the hospital or nursing home, little effort is made to help a patient maintain any control of his environment. Routine doings are imposed upon him and self-responsibility is eliminated. When to eat, to sleep, to awaken, where to go, when one can go, are sharply circumscribed. Who can visit and when, is limited. Children and pets are not allowed. Foods are curtailed. Medicines are controlled and getting in touch with the doctor depends on nurse intermediaries. Tests continue to be ordered for unexplained reasons, breakfasts withheld with little or no explanations. During these times and with these maneuvers, little time is devoted to understanding the feelings and conflicts of the dying. The goal is often not to work through the meaning of dying but to act only as if dying will be prevented. The medical and nursing staffs often create barriers that prevent the patient from voicing and thus sharing in his self-doubts. The patient who needs authority figures, medical and nursing support and in-hospital care, is assumed to need nothing else.

For the individual who must regress and give up self-control and responsibility in illness, the institution both supports and promotes further regression. As part of the regressed behavior, consideration of a patient's rights and the need to openly discuss the meaning of his illness and of his potential dying are frequently ignored. Instead, patients are frequently treated to encouragement and a pat on the back in response to an initiating effort to deal honestly with their personal feelings. After a while, many change their styles of communication and focus only on bodily complaints such as diarrhea or constipation.[1] Patients often come to respect the fact that there are few if any people in their environments with whom they can safely discuss the deep tensions within.

Death is not appropriate in today's medical view. The dying patient finds himself institutionalized and completely out of control of his limited life's activities. We hear arguments as to the definition of death, such as flattening of the electrical brain waves in the electroencephalograph, but this is clearly more mechanical than philosophic. The recently dead, as a reservoir of organs for another living body, require a definition of their status for the purpose of transplantation. Needless to say, when the interest in the dead is for organ parts, the fear is that too little struggle may be made for living. But in general, the meaning of death as an irreducible argument in life, and the rights of the dying as a special group among the living are foreign concepts to the training of most health care professionals and in the behavior of most institutions.

Undoubtedly, in some ways the fight for life is a correct professional view. Perhaps the forces of medicine must always be harnessed to life and to new technologic ways of prolonging it and salvaging it for the individual patient. But if only that view is acceptable, the question must arise as to who should have the right and the power to apply life-extending technologies in a one-way battle? Should such decisions be in the hands of technologists? There is always an extraordinary danger in allowing ultimate decisions to be made by a professional group who possess a singular methodological scheme for affecting a particular solution to a problem. If the decision for or against war, on a political level, is too important to trust to the generals, certain decisions in life and death in illness may be too important to be left to the technical physician.

For a man to face his personal death, especially in the slow dying from a fatal illness, is difficult at best. The medical care system often behaves as if such confrontation is impossible. The medical establishment frequently assumes that the patient's sole desire is to get better even if only for a few days or weeks. Since this position is taken as truth and since the physician knows best as to the treatment necessary to accomplish this goal, he oftentimes feels that he is in the best position to make all the decisions.

Furthermore, physicians are usually convinced that the modern patient and his family, especially in urban America, willingly or even desperately, turn over their faith completely to him and fully concur in all advice given. In some ways this assumption is correct. When communities were more stable and family physicians more frequent in number, and fewer elaborate technical facilities were available, decisions had to be made more in partnership. Patients and doctors knew together when *nothing more* could be medically done. Both could then aim for relief of symptoms and complaints, and a feeling of *safe passage* could be sought. The providing for a safe passage was considered a major medical skill.

Dr. Jacob Bigelow, addressing a group of medical students some hundred years ago, put a physician's duties in the following order— "to diagnose, to initiate a treatment, to offer relief of symptoms, and to provide safe passage."[2] The more the physician knew the patient, the more he could fulfill those obligations. A safe passage implied a mutual confidence and trust between patient and physician that allowed the sick to feel that all that could be done to save had been done, and that anxiety would be diminished, even unto death.

With the growth of hospitals, the development of technical medicine, the depletion of community-based physicians, and the elaboration of specialization, fewer and fewer patients are really known to their physicians. The patient easily becomes the disease process and decisions tend to be made on that basis alone. A vast array of medical potentials exist, and new research programs are elaborating new possibilities continuously. The average patient and family are often bewildered by the potential possibilities for treatments, and there is a dirth of trusted counselors whose advice can be warmly accepted. A large part of the clinical experimentation programs is based on these grounds, namely that the decisions to be made are only for the disease process, in that patients and families expect something, and that patients cannot face dying and wish to turn themselves over completely and dependently to their physicians. Medical technology is the ultimate design for disease.

Many physicians tend to enjoy the position of being the authoritarian figure in charge of a patient and being expected to make all decisions. They may certainly explain to patient and family what they intend to do and why, but they fully expect the patient to go along with the decision. The specialist especially, is the expert who may well belive in his own expertise, and expects the patient to do so as well.

Needless to say, to a certain degree, this confidence and capability is both warranted and needed, for the patient and family expect the best expertise to be available to them. Within the limitation of the knowledge possessed by any specialist, the mutual respect for that capability produces a better end result. The problem with the dying patient is that he is dying, but the expertise is struggling against the event itself. The end result is often a medical denial of the dying process, which circumscribes the patient or his family, from participating as an active partner or decision maker in his own dying.[3] Again, this is not to romanticize the dying process, nor to imply that all patients or even the majority, truly wish to confront and control events around the dying experience. There has been extensive reporting of the ability of the human mind to deny unpleasant events, and certainly many patients with a fatal illness will deny to others, and even to themselves, the fatal implications of their illness. But the closer to dying a person comes, the more readily it seems he can confront the fact of dying.

Sick people are often frightened and are dependent on the care and help of a physician. The trouble with too authoritarian a physician is that he issues an implied threat when he makes a decision for a patient, namely that if the patient does not accept this decision, not only is there "nothing more to do," but "I will have nothing more to do with you." The implication of retribution and abandonment is extremely distressing to sick people, and of sufficient pressure to force a patient or his family, to accept a treatment about which he might otherwise have doubts.

Certainly most people with fatal illness, given a choice, would opt for life rather than death. Given even a small chance for a cure or even a temporary remission, they might take the side effects and consequences of a treatment in order to get living time. The issue under discussion is not the desire for life but the freedom to confront death, to openly participate in decision making, to feel in control of one's destiny, rather than being forced to go along with someone else's decisions. There are many people who are only too anxious to turn over all responsibility to physicians, but there are many who struggle for the right of free choice.

Nurses tend to know this better than physicians. It is the nurse who is apt to spend time with the patient talking about his feelings and attitudes toward his illness and toward his doctor. Nurses, when given the chance, will often describe patients who are afraid to ask the doctor questions because "the physician is always running" or because "he is too busy" or because "when he wants me to know something, he'll tell me." In many of these instances, even though a patient blames the physician for not having time to truly talk, the person is protecting himself from having to confront the issues squarely, and it is he who shies away from open viewing and sharing with his doctor. But this is not always true, and many physicians do not give patients a chance to discuss delicate matters.

Many are quite willing to go along with anything directed at them, including a friendly pat on the back that "I'll take care of things" by the physician. Doctors rate such people as "good" patients. Such good patients often turn angrily on nurses, social workers, or their families to relieve an anguish, uncertainty or fear that is lurking beneath the surface, and not allowed out in the physician-patient exchange. Physicians generally, tend to be minimally aware of the frightening struggles going on inside their patients. They want, or prefer, their charges to be compliant, gratified, unquestioning and accepting.

The issue of new, experimental drugs for fatally ill persons is a thorny one. One would hope that physicians would not administer a new drug to a patient without the full conviction that the patient has a reasonably good chance to benefit from the material. This should be especially true with drugs that cause many unpleasant or possibly life-shortening effects, such as hair loss, blistering of mouth, nausea, vomiting, skin rashes, etc. Unfortunately, this is not always true. There often is a great pressure exerted, especially from research agencies, to learn something about the new drug. There is also a strong feeling that a patient with a fatal illness is obliged to contribute himself to a program of experimentation for the good of mankind, so that knowledge can grow and at some future date another person might be benefitted.

If a particular patient wished to contribute himself to such research, he should certainly be allowed and encouraged to do so. However, many patients are seduced into these clinical research programs by either a promise or a threat. The promise is that this new agent may just be the "answer for you." The threat is of the physician's disapproval and abandonment if the patient refuses. The researcher may argue that offering these new agents extends hope to the patient, and a continued interest in him as a patient. I believe that most sick patients want some element of hope to be offered to them, but not in the form of a delusion. A person cannot continually be disappointed in the name of hope without feeling diminished. Hope may be preferably expressed in trust in a continued relationship and a safekeeping. When a physician believes in a right to use patients and offers seductions to obtain compliance, he may well be forcing his patient into a quiet despair and resignation rather than helping him find meaning in his life.

Although the federal government now insists on an informed consent document that a patient or family must sign in order to participate in a clinical experiment with a new or unusual drug or treatment, such consent is not the equal to free and uncoerced participation. Too often an individual's frailty is taken advantage of, and too infrequently is the somewhat recalcitrant patient allowed to doubt or say no, and still feel safe. The patient is seldom allowed options, for options are seldom truly offered. To be able to say no and still feel that the physician will care and continue to look after needs and offer relief, is the essence of feeling in safe passage. Many patients will quickly say yes to any chance at life. It is those who might wish to say no who need safety.

Once again, what is under discussion is a person's right and freedom to be in control of his life processes, especially as he moves towards his individual death. I am not insisting that every person have courage, style and faith in himself. Good medical care begins at the patient's bedside and accepts the individual for what he is. If a patient with a fatal illness is psychologically forced to deny his illness or to deny his closeness to death, he should not be forced to face death openly. If a person wishes to become completely dependent on his physician or the institution for care and safekeeping, and wishes all decisions to be made for him, he should be accepted in that dependent role. But where a person wishes help and not domination, guidance and not total dependence, participation in decision making around his life rather than just following orders, all effort should be made to encourage him towards such behavior. For it is in self control and the right to participate that dignity resides. The fear of abandonment, retribution and unnecessary pain can easily prevent people from expressing their inner anguish, and feelings of belittlement. Trying to look good to a physician in order to please him and keep his protective graces nearby, need not be developed into complete self-sacrifice. The aim, in helping dying people, should be to prosper courage, to prosper self-esteem, to further acceptance of the life that was and is. The goal should be to help people die well.

The question is not really whether new knowledge should or should not be pursued, nor whether improvements in the treatment of fatal illnesses such as cancer should or should not be researched. Diseases such as cancer fill the hearts of most persons with fear and terror, and eradication is highly to be desired. But we must face several critical questions as we encourage a control of disease. First, towards what end are we moving with these objectives, and at what price? Is our aim eradication of cancer so that men can die of less frightening illness? Is our aim the eradication of all illness in the young and middle-aged so that only the elderly will die, a completion of the trend already begun in this century? Is our aim the eradication of all illness and aging so that men will be corporeally immortal?

Secondly, are people with fatal illnesses to be considered only as subjects for learning? Do the dying owe something to future generations, and what is it that they owe? Should we demand that they owe something, or should we allow them to reject any such debt? Thirdly, and perhaps most importantly, do all people find the only meaning to their lives and to their dying an extension of life itself? And if so, at any cost? Or are there other basic human issues such as faith, love, and concern for others that need to be understood and prospered to help people accept a meaning to their lives at the end? Fourthly, can one have dignity in dying unless one feels in control of events in his life, and has a sense of self-esteem even at the end? Does a person have the right to have something to say as to the manner and style of his living and dying, or are we to conclude that it is all in the hands of the medical profession and the institutions? Fifthly, is our aim the eradication of suffering or can we help people to rise above their suffering to a yet higher level of understanding and humaneness?

Since dying today has become mostly a medical problem, the struggle for improving the dying process must be through improving the medical definition of the problem, and to applying new areas of knowdelge and resources to the problem. Medical behavior does not exist in a vacuum, it is an arm of the public's willing and needing. The issue surely requires definition as to what is really wanted. Can our society help the ill to live and die well through their last, fatal illness, or is the battle to be solely for survival? Can we be prepared to understand the agonies of today's dying person so that he can be helped to live his maximum in whatever his time is? Modern medicine has progressed so that people now live longer with their chronic illnesses before death. But they also face the dilemma of taking longer to die. In psychologic, sociologic and economic terms, the price is frequently expensive and must be so understood.

[1]Abrams, Ruth D.: The patient with cancer—his changing pattern of communication. *New England Journal of Medicine, 274*:317-322, 1966.

[2]Bigelow, Jacob: *Brief Expositions of Rationale Medicine.* Boston, Philips, Sampson, 1958. I am indebted to Dr. Avery Weisman for this reference.

[3]Weisman, Avery: *On Dying and Denying.* New York, Behavioral Publications, 1972.

CHAPTER V

EUTHANASIA — A PEACEFUL DEATH

THE TERM "euthanasia" has come to imply a contract for the termination of life in order to avoid unnecessary suffering at the end of a fatal illness. The implication is that if an individual is dying and suffering excessively, further extension of life should not be forced on that person just so that life itself is preserved. Euthanasia's proponents argue that a person should have the right to control the ending of his life if he has a fatal illness, and if the only future for him is suffering. For some, euthanasia has come to mean "mercy killing" in that an individual requests some form of medication that would end his life. The physician, or perhaps a delegated authority, would be responsible for the administration of the medication. An overt pact for terminating life would exist, and this would be termed "active" euthanasia. For the Euthanasia Society, the term implies the right of an individual to control a dignified death by requesting that no extraordinary means be used to extend biologic life when death from a fatal illness is close. "The "living will" of the Euthanasia Society reads as follows:

TO MY FAMILY, MY PHYSICIAN, MY CLERGYMAN, MY LAWYER:

If the time comes when I can no longer take part in decisions for my own future, let this statement stand as the testament of my wishes.

If there is no reasonable expectation of my recovery from physical or mental disability, I, _____ request that I be allowed to die and not be kept alive by artificial means or heroic gestures. Death is as much a reality as birth, growth, maturity and old age—it is the one certainty. I do not fear death as much as I fear the indignity of deterioration, dependence and hopeless pain. I ask that drugs be mercifully administered to me for terminal suffering even if they hasten the moment of death.

This request is made after careful consideration. Although this document is not legally binding, you who care for me will, I hope, feel morally bound to follow its mandate. I recognize that it places a heavy burden of responsibility upon you, and it is with the intention of sharing that responsibility and of mitigating any feelngs of guilt that this statement is made. *I wish to die dignity that's all*

Signed---

Date--

Witnessed by:

This document is essentially a passive request, and depends on moral persuasion. The physician is not legally bound to accept the patient's wishes.[1]

Euthanasia implies a dependency. The ill person is essentially incapable of ending his life by self-destruction, either because of the nonavailability of resources, or because of an inability to self-terminate due to physical or psychologic incapacity. There have been a number of descriptions of suicides among people seriously ill, even hospitalized and in weakened conditions, implying that where there is that will and determination, the physical manner of killing oneself is available. In one situation that I am aware of, a patient in a first floor room tied one end of a bedsheet to the side rail of the bed, the other around his neck, and pushed himself out the window. The inability of most people to take their own lives rests more on a social and psychological constraint, even in the face of severe disease, overwhelming pain and frailty, and imminent death. A compact with a physician for the ending of one's life passively or actively is in recognition of this extraordinary barrier to suicide that operates in the life force of most people. It is also a testament to the existence of abiding faith and a sense of reliance that a safeguarding force can be trusted to judge correctly when no further improvement is possible and only continuing agony remains. In a way, euthanasia in this sense is a combination of an ultimate trust on an authoritarian figure's judgment, as well as an insistence that a rational man has the rational right to request an end of his life under certain circumstances.

Physicians, nurses, lawyers and many lay people have difficulty with concepts of modern day euthanasia. This difficulty appears to rest on ethical, religious and political grounds. One argument appears to be that a person, in general, cannot be trusted to enter into such covenants because both the "victim" and the "executioner" may accrue personal gains from such an arrangement, and that these gains must be protected against. The victim, for example, might not be terminally sick at all, but merely tired of life, or in psychopathologic terms, seeking death as a resolution for life's problems that might well be resolved in another fashion. The medical profession should not act as legal suicide-helpers. In a religious way, there is a taint of ungodliness in such euthanasia, for it is against the will and design of God for one to end his life prematurely. His life does not really belong to him, but to God who gave it, and it must be God and God alone who takes it back. This argument has held for the Catholic and orthodox Jewish faiths for many centuries. The church refused to allow the liturgies and sacred solemnities for the dead to be intoned if death was by suicide, and burial would not be allowed in hallowed ground. Grace was absent in either self-destruction, or even in a premature wish for death. This position of punishment has been eased in modern times, principally by accepting the concept of psychopathology, which fundamentally relieves man of his responsibility for self-will. Suicide, in this sense, must be pathologic, for only the mentally ill would want to kill themselves. The ill person seeking death through compact bears some of that old stain of suicide, for only God has the right to terminate life in His due time. The argument then, is that men must be guarded against the potential fulfillment of pathologic wishes. Society must be guarded against the self-indulgent possibility of killing oneself, or of getting oneself into premature death actively or passively.

The executioner must also clearly be guarded against. For some, he would be playing God's role, and no man must be allowed such proximity. Besides, how could anyone be sure, even if the most legally supervised of compacts had been arranged by a patient in sound mind, that the physician might not be tempted on occasion by an eager relative to exercise his "killing" role prematurely. Or perhaps, the patient might have changed his or her mind toward the end of life, and must be protected from an overly ambitious physician, or an overly taxed one, who might see in the euthanasia agreement an easy way to be rid of a burdensome treatment problem. There might well be some gain, such as money, by hastening a death, and such possibility requires an active restraint.

But perhaps even more prominent an argument is the demand that the physician be always and only on the side of life and that death must always be the enemy. One slip away from this absolute position, so the argument goes, might result in larger and easier slips, endangering a social responsibility. For the individual, life is sacrosanct in its corporeal being, and the physician must always stand on the side of that life. This argument is enriched by many anecdotes and parables regarding the occasional individual who has been close to death, even in coma, for weeks or months only to recover. No one can ever be totally sure, not even for the emaciated terminal person.

Similar kinds of feelings are frequently present in nurses who harbor the sentiment that they do not want to be the individual giving the last injection of a needed and long-used narcotic to a dying patient, for then they can be interpreted as being an executioner. The nurse also stands primarily for life. Besides which, nurses and physicians are held accountable for their actions regarding patients. Reports must be made to supervisors, to chiefs, to administrators. Professionals have been trained not to give narcotics to certain patients, such as unresponsive ones, or to those with labored or slowed respiration rates. To administer an injection or a drug such as morphine to a semiresponsive, dying patient, often flies in the face of careful training, and a supervisor or chief, far from the patient's bedside and filled with the righteousness of rules and regulations, might raise a terrible row. One could even be fired!

Passive withdrawal of life-supporting systems such as tubes and intravenous feedings simply to allow a person to die unencumbered by technical artifices is also subject to authoritative scrutiny. What a supervisor or colleague might say is frequently given considerable weight in the decision-making process of a medical staff member. A professional must account for his actions, especially in an institution, and a patient's private wishes often become secondary to institutional policy.

This present concept of euthanasia is a somewhat altered derivative of a long-standing, valued, historic position, namely, that the physician should help his patient die well. The word "euthanasia" was apparently known to and used by the ancient Romans in that same sense that it has been understood until this century, namely that the act of dying should be peaceful, and that medical art should assist in its accomplishment.

One of the clearest statements in this regard came from Sir Francis Bacon, writing in the seventh century, about the duties of the physician.[2] He stated thus, "I esteem it to be clearly the office of a physician, not only to restore health but also to mitigate the pains and torments of diseases and not only when such mitigation of pain as a dangerous symptom helps and conduces to recovery, but also when all hope of recovery being gone, it serves only to make a fair and easy passage from life." It was for this felicity, a fair and easy passage from life, that the Roman Emperor Augustus Caesar was said to have so earnestly prayed and which likewise, was the prayer and indeed the manner of the death of the Roman, Antonius Pius, described not so much like death as like falling into a deep and pleasant sleep.

For the physician of another time, actively helping someone to die was seen as a positive role. In 1826, a German physician, Karl Friedrich Marx, published a dissertation on the concepts of euthanasia, reinforcing the position that the physician had the duty to work towards an easy and peaceful death for his patient.[3a] In this sense, euthanasia was not seen simply as a compact for killing, but the enunciation of the right to and need for a peaceful and good death.

Marx had no compunction about using medicines freely to accomplish euthanasia and indeed, it is clear from the many writings of past centuries, that liberal use of potions, concoctions and medicines were indicated to help men in trouble die peacefully. Marx went further in his dissertation, urging physicians beyond the dispensing of medicines to the administering of some kind of higher comfort, for as he wrote, "whoever refuses this duty and assigns it solely to the priests, deprives himself of the most noble and rewarding aspect of his work." Marx's psychology was steeped in religion. As a member of a religious community, this physician maintained an orderly and sacred definition of life and death and performed his tasks as a Christian priest and physician with an easy unity that was met with an easy acceptance by his patients. His task of comforting was obviously made lighter by this sense of religious and medical correlation, not only for himself, but for those under his care. In his publication in the year 1826, Marx posed the question, "why should not man, with his intellect mastering so many problems, find and produce some skillful contrivance for the care of the dying? The physician is not expected to have a remedy for death, but for skillful alleviation of suffering." The art of euthanasia, in these terms, was the "obstetrics of the soul."[3b]

Clearly, our secular, pluralistic society lacks such an easy congruence of the biologic, the psychologic and the sacred. Both physician and patient today are expected to behave in a rationalistic, rather than religious or ritualistic, manner. Today it is primarily to the scientific physician, and not to the religionist, that the operational aspects of death are brought. Modern medical psychology avoids the issues of faith and religiosity and it is the rare physician who is able, willing or daring to bring God to the bedside. Besides, we do not know how many patients welcome God at their deathbeds. In general, minister and physician are separate entities and when one enters, the other leaves. It is usually the physician who preempts the priest. All too often heard from the young physician in the modern hospital setting is something like, "excuse me, Sir, I have something important to do," shoving the minister out the door. In a recent student seminar on the dying person held at a prestigious New England medical school, during a ninety-minute discussion in which a psychiatrist and physician presided, religion and the role of the ministry were not mentioned, even one time.

Not only is the art of euthanasia, in the sense of a good and peaceful death, absent from the conceptualization of today's health scheme, it is absent from the thinking of most citizens and most families, unless good and peaceful becomes translated into quick and painless. Terms such as "death with dignity" are often heard, but the art and manner of its accomplishment are poorly reckoned.

The concept that the art of euthanasia should be applied to life and illness seemed to fade as a positive force in medicine with the growth of science and biology. The vast gains in medical technology and medical caregiving during the past fifty to seventy years has promoted the notion that in general, the patient now dies when treatment has nothing more to offer. The idea of a treatment for dying seems no longer pertinent. Of course there are physicians who practice warm and effective personal care, and who have developed a personal style to help patients die. There is not, however, an educational demand that the art of euthanasia be a basic required skill for caregivers.

Our society, with medicine as its subordinate, must continually examine its goals and objectives, and the time is long overdue for a reexamination of the value, the meaning and the place of death. The problem is not unique to the twentieth century. Marx was critical of certain physicians in his time who, "once they see the expected result of their treatment to be wanting, and once they are convinced of the hopelessness of the patient's case, start to lose interest themselves, thinking they have all but discharged their duties if they have made ample use of the therapeutic means, believing they are dealing with a disease, not with a human being." This nineteenth century physician urged that there are:

> three points on which the doctor's efforts to discharge this sacred duty to help a patient, so that the last breath of passing which can be observed, may be light, and not dreadful to those left behind. First that he, (the physician) by every means possible, alleviate the patient's condition through foresight and guidance; second, that he avoid and remove everything that might increase the patient's pain and suffering; third, that he cheer the patient's soul and mind with 'gracious and convincing comfort.'

What Marx had in mind, in this statement of the interpersonal psychology, is revealed when discussing the physician's role as death draws closer:

> as he (the physician) knows from experience how to alleviate the supreme anguish of the patient's mind by conferring confidence to the dying about the safe and secure future of those to be left behind, his wife, children, dearest stakes in life, he will put forth his best efforts in this kind of comforting. Likewise he will assure the doubtful and agitated of an honorable funeral and a not-too-hasty interment. Finally, as a

truthful interpreter of nature, he will relieve the troubled from his
fear of complete extinction by giving him hope of immortality and of
everlasting life of the soul.

But Marx, religious as he was, argued deliberately against hastening
death and disdained that a sense of mercy, or another's request, should
be allowed to sway the physician into hastening death.

I have quoted liberally from Marx, not with the intent of arguing
pro or con the present definition of euthanasia, but to give some
perspective of that other quality defined by the past usage of the term,
the pursuit of a peaceful and dignified death. It may well be that our
present distortion of the old term derives from the regrettable awareness that present day medical caregiving, especially in large, urban
institutions, is incapable of defining and accepting peaceful death,
but is intent on forcing the individual into an endless battle in which
only a pact-for-mercy can be construed as peaceful. If the difficulties
existing in institutional care, and in depersonalized biologic science
were confronted and reconciled with some of the great advances in
modern medicine, a peaceful ending, really synonymous with dignified
living to the end, might well be the common lot of man.

Peace at the end implies an acceptance of a life's meaning at the
time of life's ending, not simply a resignation from a futile life. A
fulfilled life implies a strong personal ego and a sense of self-esteem
and worth. To be readily apparent at the end of life, these commodities of the human condition should exist during life and be the
goal of life itself. Can one talk of dignity in dying if dignity has
been absent in life? Can one talk of the maintenance of self-esteem
in dying, if such has been denied to an individual by the nature of
his existence? Can a man die of his life if he never truly owned his
life?

There is a much needed operational task in helping the dying to
find peace, especially in the absence of a strong religious consola-
tional belief. It is the absence that forces the problem into a psychologic and sociologic mold. The physician of old may have been
comfortable in equating psychology with liturgic pronouncement.
The modern problem in the absence of such implied consolation
forces us to look to behavioral science as a potential form of human
consolation.

Viktor Frankl, an Austrian psychiatrist and proponent of a form of psychotherapy termed logotherapy, has defined the basic tragedy of human existence by the triad of pain, suffering and death.[4] What is critical to Frankl's view of tragedy is not the avowed existence of death but the attitude that is taken by the suffering individual towards his fate. The fate is there, but for Frankl, it is what man does with it, what attitude he assumes in dealing with it, that creates either a victory or a defeat in the face of suffering, without obliterating the suffering itself. Logotherapy is a form of existential or spiritual support and consolation, an effort to help an individual sufferer find meaning and peace in the confrontation with his unmitigated fate. The dying person is often in sore need of such consolation, if peace is to emerge.

Other manners and style of reaching such peace for different people may well be needed, and a search for understanding the many complicated interactions around dying and living requires continual research and observation.

What is needed today is a design for legitimatizing death in our midst in a manner that allows consolations, or support in dying, to be available to the sick. The creation of any design for helping the dying to die well, peacefully and in control of their lives is far from an easy matter. The care given to the sick has been institutionalized and professionalized, and one outcome has been to hide, to deny, or diminish dying as a personal event. Institutions and professionals are resistant to change. But too many social changes have occurred to look for a rapid de-institutionalization, such as returning the care of the terminally sick and dying to their families and homes. There may be few modern citizens who would find advantages in such de-institutionalization. The present social existence of small nuclear families, small nuclear homes, quick and easy mobility, urban concentration of population, and money-for-services exchanges, works against a simple reordering of home and personal care at the end of life. The care of the sick and dying has become institutionalized, and we must proceed to look at issues in this light.

The primary question is a philosophic one and begins with the right and need for death to exist, and the right to consciously and knowingly participate in the events inherent in personal dying and death. Such a question is not meant to diminish the excruciating anxiety and fear of death that exists in most, if not all men, as well as the fact that even most fatally ill individuals exhibit a certain degree or dimension of denying that personal death is close at hand. The fear of death, and the facing of death are not the same questions, and the denial of an oncoming death appears only seldom to be the only psychological stance of the fatally ill. As indicated earlier, there is a positive, protective value of a fear in general, although such fear has never interfered with sanctified death for a cause or ideal. Death can be elected heroically, as a suicide mission in wartime, or voluntarily surrendering one's place in a lifeboat (in those romantic days of ocean-going ships) to a weaker person. Men overcome fear of death to give their lives for a cause. Some may wish to argue that all such behavior is indicative of a sick mind, but such argument would diminish man to a bag of cringing, self-protecting sentiments, and would be contrary to the known heights of selflessness recorded in the thought and actions of many in the past. Dying from a disease is obviously not heroic nor elected. Nevertheless, fear of death is not a condition of inability to face one's death in illness, nor argument against being alive to the issues and meanings of dying, and living, while approaching death.

For most people, there is little opportunity for a personal style and manner in facing one's dying. The term "style" would imply that a person is playing a role, or a part, in this action. To have style requires that there be one. A style of dying, if I can be excused for using a somewhat theatrical form, relates not only to psychological stages but to a meaning that an individual gives to his life and death.

The literature of previous centuries often depicted the great death bed scenes where a patriarch lay dying, surrounded by a large, sometimes loving, family, and made pronouncements as to what he wished for his various sons, daughters, nephews, nieces and others. There was a grand style in such dying. One could sense dignity, courage, love and concern as part of the behavior of the dying person, describing his confrontation with the end of life. In such depictions, man is seen as more than a simple mechanical arrangement of organs, cells and instincts. He is a human, capable of going beyond himself, capable of transcending himself through the love and concern of others, through the belief in ideals, through a search for a meaning in his life and beyond his life. Such a transcending human being has considerable style. But he often needs an environment where such style is encouraged, or supported, as a positive value. Such style can become its own consolation—the comforting of others who must go on living.

Considerable attention has been given recently to the psychological stages of the dying person.[5] Such terms as shock, denial, anger, bargaining, depression, resignation and acceptance have been well described. Such terms apply not only to the crisis of dying, but to many critical events besetting an individual's life. Certainly to learn the news that one has a fatal illness and may be close to dying, can be shocking, although there are many who have been suspicious of such a possibility for a long time prior to being given a diagnosis. For such people, confirmation in words is not unexpected. Anger, bargaining, depression are inherent in all felt injustices, and disease and dying is in an injustice of some kind, to many, perhaps excepting the very elderly. Resignation, and/or acceptance are probably not the last terms in a series of stages, but are part of the basic human personality framework that allows for an overall behavioral rapprochement with assaults of any kind. Feeling helpless or resigned in the face of a calamity is a frequent human condition. Accepting the reality of a problem and mobilizing resources to deal with it is quite another matter. The final acceptance of death, for the dying, in allowing death to peacefully come, is often the last moment of a longer existing acceptance of mortality in the human condition of illness, and not just a last minute evolution. Acceptance allows for an integration of the past history of an individual as having both meaning and presence, and also allows for the transcendence of that individual from concern for only self, to a deeper concern for the others who will go on living beyond his time.

Psychological terms, as listed above, are mostly negative in their implication. Such terms do not help us understand such concepts as will, love and courage, concepts which transcend simplistic analytic descriptions, but nevertheless forces operating in people, directing the manner and style with which life's issues are faced and resolved. The quality and quantity of such human sentiments determine how a man will face his dying, but even these terms are not full enough. People must interact with others in their environment and such interaction can support or cripple resolve, courage and dignity by enhancing or diminishing a person's sense of self-worth and self-esteem. The truly brave and truly loving may be able to conquer even in the face of a diminishing human environment, but many people with an adequate but not absolute sense of themselves need support in order to feel esteemed and worthy, especially when injured or damaged by disease. It is such support that goes into the make up of consolation.

A great deal has also been written about the process of denial in dying[6]. We can describe such denial as a mental state in which the fatally ill do not outwardly acknowledge the seriousness of their condition, and insist that they are improving, or holding their own, when in fact they are worsening unto death. The definition of the term implies that one individual must indicate to another how he interprets his condition. This means, of course, that the second individual must be able to communicate accurately with the first. If the second individual does not want to hear what the first is saying, or is himself denying the gravity of the situation, then an accurate communication cannot exist.

Observations of dying patients by a number of physicians, sociologists and nurses, support the notion that most patients are aware of their dying at the same time that they may wish to avoid excessive detailing of the dying process.[7] Denying and acknowledging often fluctuate in intensity in the same individual.

When, and if, the person or persons attending a dying individual, wish to deny to the ill person an opportunity to acknowledge the proximity of death, and an opportunity to openly explore fears, concerns or fantasies, that individual is often deprived of needed support and consolation, and may be forced into deepening depression and loneliness. Such a state could be called denial, but it actually is an environmental denial and not a patient denial.

The movement of a sick man to a state of euthanasia, a truly peaceful death, requires that his sense of self-worth be allowed to exist or to be encouraged to emerge. This cannot be accomplished if the sick individual feels a sense of helplessness over whatever remaining controllable phenomena exist in his world. As a person becomes physically weaker, control over his bodily processes becomes obviously less. He just cannot do many things for himself, and walking a short distance or even dressing himself may become a difficult chore. Simple, routine daily life functions have to be done for him, or he has to be helped to do them. The opportunities for exercising choice or control over daily events become more and more infrequent.

As long as awareness exists, the dying person must confront these exigencies, namely the excrutiating dissolution of person and the loss of an ability to interact helpfully with others. The loss of this capacity to *do* for others, so much an ingrained characteristic of the role performer as mother, father, brother, sister or simply person, easily becomes equated with self-worthlessness. A sense of worthlessness is incompatible with self-dignity and eventuates into helplessness, resignation, clingingness, anger or despair. If added to these feelings of worthlessness is economic destitution of oneself, especially of one's loved ones in the future, and a conviction that one did nothing with his life but wasted it, the sense of despairing burdensomeness can be overwhelming.

Courage allows a man to be what he ideally wishes to be. Courage to say no to forces operating to take over control of one's world allows a man to live in the ideal of himself, in the image he has painted of what he would like to be, or what he would like to show to others. Courage does not deny fear, especially the fear of dissolution. Courage allows a man to control his place and options in the limited world of sickness. Love allows a person to make decisions about himself that show consideration for others. Love is not the antithesis of fear, but a way to live through and diminish fear. In his book *Man's Search for Meaning,* Viktor Frankl attempts to explain phenomena that allowed a man to survive brutality, illness, starvation and a sense of inhumaneness as experienced in the Nazi concentration camps of the 1940's.[8] The one human ingredient that emerges as the life preserving force is love, love of another person, of an ideal, of a labor. For Frankl, love gave a man the strength to invest his meager life with ongoingness. Love is no different for the dying. Love allows the dying person to find meaning in his last days and to feel purpose and goal in a dignified dying.

For the typical dying person today, such human passions operate in a climate of institutional rituals, barriers and professional assumptions rather than in a geography of home and family. The very strong have a courage that no institution or authority can break. The very strong can have love that is inspirational going beyond events that mortify through bodily changes, loss of bodily control, and damaging disease or treatments. The very strong, in essence, have dignity despite what happens to them.

Most of us are not so fashioned. Most of us feel significantly diminished when we feel we have become objects in the sickness world, rather than valued persons. A recent publication by a man dying of a brain tumor takes extraordinary account of this objectivization.[9] Discussing such events as his admission to a hospital on a Friday with nothing scheduled over a holiday weekend, experiences with enforced wheel chair use, signing financial obligation documents of unknown magnitude, undergoing multiple medical examinations by students so that they could learn something about his illness without either discussing such examinations or requesting permission from him for them, he concludes with;

> being a patient is one thing, but being an object is even less than being a patient. And I began to feel not only the fear of this unknown dread thing that I have (his illness), but an anger and a resentment of, goddammit, I'm a human being and I want to be treated like one. And feeling that if I expressed that anger, I could be retaliated against, because I'm in a very vulnerable position.

Fear of the unknown, of disease, of dying, of death, are all real enough. Feeling that one cannot humanely communicate, or be humanely considered, in institutional ritual or professional performance, immediately diminishes one's sense of esteem. The point of this is that to be helped to die with peace and dignity, one must be in an environment that fosters feelings of concern, worth, purpose, meaning and trust. The person with a fatal illness needs to feel supported with grace in living through his last period of time.

We must be careful to be aware of such psychological processes, as anger, but not to insist that all behavior exhibited by the sick can be reduced to neat psychologic terms. The gentleman mentioned above could easily be described as angry at his fate or angry at his state of illness, and be seen to be projecting his anger into events, circumstances and people. To an extent, that might be true; but not to recognize that the sick are sensitive to events in their environment, would be to excuse all personnel and institutional insensitivity, and to place all responsibility on psychology. This is patently not true.

And it is here that we need to examine the roles of communion, compassion, empathy, consolation and trust as contradistinctive to biological examination, exploration, treatment and seduction. We must look at ways that help an individual feel in control of himself and feel safe in passing through fearful portals. For the professional, and for the institution, it means a trust in the innate strength of most people to confront this area of human crisis in illness and dying, and help them to be a participant in decisions which affect the manner of their living and the style of their dying.

Translating euthanasia into an operational design should emphasize the right to a dignified living in that period of time left to a person, within the confines and limitations imposed by the illness. In order for such dignified living to be present, those professionals and family members caring for the individual patient must understand empathetically the perceptions of damage inherent in illness, and the need to support the human esteem of a sick person. While search continues for new and effective anti-disease treatments, reemphasis on the needs of consolation, communion and support must be made, and an integration of such concepts as *meaning*, into the policy of caretaking fostered. Helping a person to cope with his tragedy should become a critical design in the management of fatal illness and dying. I would like to amplify these concepts by looking at the problem of the cancer patient. There are many different fatal illnesses, and the same principles of support and consolation can apply to them all.

Cancer, however, remains the disease that is most terrifying to most Americans, not just because of its fatalness, but because of the stresses induced as one perceives marked changes in body image and identity. These changes are inherent in the disease itself and in what is done in treatment. People speak of cancer as loathsome, smelly, foul, disgusing, and as the disease develops, patients may visualize these characteristics as now applying not only to the disease, but to their total selves.[10] Feelings of disgust for oneself are frequent, and words such as "shame" are frequently heard. Family and friends often share in the sentiment. People with cancer tend to encourage social isolation, and those around them often have a great need to withdraw. In some ways, this withdrawal is forced because of the conviction the sufferer has that he is disgusting or revolting, and that people will have little but contempt for him now. If there is disfiguring or open malodorous wounds, these feelings of a personal disgust can be easily understood. Withdrawing protects one against having to face another's contempt, but also, unfortunately, reinforces a terrible sense of worthlessness.

Not all cancer is fatal, and many people are curable by modern surgical, radiotherapeutic and chemotherapeutic methods. But even when "fatalness" is removed for any singular patient, frequently this has been accomplished by a disfiguring surgery that may so dislocate a person's sense of self-security, that living is really psychologic suffering. The younger woman for example, who has placed a great deal of psychologic investment in her breasts as a source of womanness, beauty and sexual attraction, can be grievously wounded when a radical breast removal operation cures her of cancer. A prosthesis may serve to grant normalcy to the outer world, but deep inner doubts may be incapacitating, especially if she perceives the man in her life as less attentive or rejecting. For the single or divorced woman, such an operation may have devastating consequences for future social relations. An operation on the bowel, resulting in a colostomy, discharging fecal material into a bag on the abdominal wall, can be a fantastic insult to the person invested in personal cleanliness as a way of life. There are operations which result in disfigurations of the face, amputation of an extremity, alteration of the voice.

These procedures and many more, can prove to be enormous insults, even if curative, to people who see their primary bodily image dependent on that part of their anatomy. The actor, the singer, the teacher, (professional, amateur or secretly ambitious) need to be understood in terms of their psychological investment into the particular body part that now has been changed by the procedure. Many hospitals are now concerned enough about such reactions to both illness and treatment, and have organized helping teams to deal with both the patients' and family's responses to the procedure. However, such "helping teams" are far from universal and seldom exist in community hospitals or in most large city hospitals. There is great need for "colostomy clubs," "amputation clubs," and the like, composed of people who have lived through and mastered disfiguring operations to help others with similar situations.

Often the bodily image-altering treatment is not curative. The disease recurs or spreads elsewhere in the body. This may happen years after the original procedure. People look to the figure of five years as a magical number. If one can survive to that date then one is truly cured. Five years is not only no guarantee, but when looked at in another way, is rather frightening. Patients must live their lives within that block of time wondering whether each day might reveal evidence of recurrent disease. Frequently a patient or family will keep this concern closeted away and out of view as though by not discussing or considering it, the phenomenon of its being would not exist. At times such nondiscussable concern can take interesting turns.

One middle aged patient whom I had been seeing on a twice yearly basis, in follow-up after a radical mastectomy for what appeared to be a small and potentially quite curable breast cancer, gained an enormous quantity of weight over a three year period. Her complaints to me were not about cancer but about weight. She had been to several doctors and had tried various diets, but did not seem able to lose or to stop gaining weight. She disliked herself because of her appearance and was spending less and less time with friends, and more and more time at home alone. Even at home, there were increasingly fewer pleasures shared with husband and children. As we talked, images concerning cancer began to slowly emerge, and most poignantly, she revealed her interpretation that people with cancer lose weight and become thin. As long as one did not lose weight, then cancer was not threatening. Weight gaining for her had become a protective conviction that she did not have cancer, even though the shame of her weight, complicating the issue of cancer and mastectomy, were forcing her into withdrawing from usual social interrelationships.

For the patient who is not cured, but who must face recurrence of disease, the assault on one's identity and integrity may be oppressive. Not only is there no "sense" in the illness, but the whole matter becomes a bizarre joke. There may be exquisite pain in realizing the futility of the previous surgery. The meaninglessness of the previous procedures can turn to anger and rejection, not only of the physician, but of God, of family, of loved ones. It is at these moments that nothing can be trusted, and feelings of guilt, or of cosmic punishment, emerge. Such an individual can then feel intensely lonely. It is often hard for an individual to talk about such matters, for who can be trusted to listen? In such anguish of guilt, of loss of self-esteem, of loss of trust in the world, of shame and lovelessness, people often recede further into themselves. Some may continue to look to medical treatment as a magical and divine answer, although frequently with increasing doubts. Some may call this hope, and in a magical way, the hope of getting better is a sustaining force in continuing to live. But hope and despair are often two sides of a single coin, and when magical hope is thwarted one time too many, deep despair emerges.

Not all people respond to advancing illness with feelings of blame and anger, but many do. There is also a terrible feeling of helplessness in many cancer patients, a helplessness that emanates from the belief that the patient should be able to control things by working at it, but knowing full well that matters are out of his hands. This is quite different in ways, than the heart disease patient, who may feel that he can control his illness by resting, or not getting excited. The helpless feeling frequently leads to greater and greater reliance on authority-type figures like the physician. The patient can regress psychologically, looking to the authority figure as a powerful father figure. How easy it is to give up self-control and dignity in such a circumstance. It is exactly at this point that effort must be made to reestablish and support a sense of self-esteem and a sense of self-control.

This can best be done if the paternal or authoritarian physician recognizes his own leanings towards omnipotence, and the easy seductibility present in his position. Even the patient who insists that he is leaving everything in his doctor's hands, should be viewed as a man needing help to prevent total regression and dependence. While resignation through helplessness occurs often, a pressing question is whether such behavior is credited with being a normal part of dying, or if the possibility exists that there is something in the medical care system that encourages such behavior to emerge.

While it is patently true that many a person, sick with fatal illness, begins to regress psychologically from maturity to dependency, and searches for rescue in the personage of the caretakers, especially the physician, such regression is encouraged by deceit and objectivization. By the latter, I mean the process of forcing a person to fit into a particular mold, perhaps proven efficient in the care of biologic disease, but essentially robbing him of a personal sense of himself. One such deceit would be lying, or distorting a diagnosis. Every individual has the right to know what is happening to him and to his personal life from information gathered about him by another. The individual who goes to a physician for help because signs and symptoms of a disease have appeared, has the right to know what the physician comes to know.

Physicians and other professionals who feel they have the right to deny valid information from a patient usually do so on the basis of protection. The argument is given that such deception is needed in order to promote living. But in so doing, is not the inherent right of a person to decide for himself the meaning of his personal life, and also his right to confront and live that life authentically, denied? Since no man is capable of completely tailoring another's interpretation of life, (except in politically or socially totalitarian systems), is it not essential that each person with a fatal illness be allowed to examine the information pertinent to his state of illness, both in actual and symbolic terms, and to determine what his life will now mean?

I believe that each individual has an unalterable right to know that he has developed a disorder that will be fatal to him sooner or later, and that he has this right to know in a language that is clear and concise, rather than steeped in scientisms and vagaries. But the right to know, if we pose this right as a human condition, has within it enormous variance as to how truth is told.

Argument posed to the negative about such truth in communication appears based on one presumption or another regarding the need to protect a person from himself. A concerned question is raised as to just what a person would do, or what would happen, if he knew the truth? Somewhere is always the lurking suspicion that the person would be destroyed psychologically, or might in fact physically destroy himself if he knew that he had a fatal illness. Perhaps some might, but before we automatically assume that such action is wrong, we must probe a moment into the problem of suicide. Clearly, if an individual learns of an illness such as cancer, and wrongly interprets the circumstances as fatal when this is not so, a suicide based on this misinformation or misinterpretation, would be faulty for all concerned. If the price for cure is a maiming, disfiguring operation, with destruction of a highly prized psychologic image, then the act of suicide may be another issue. But let us agree that strong psychologic, and family loving support, can restore such an individual to a better self-image and less hopeless state. We can certainly plead for such restitution.

However, if an illness is fatal, and the fate irrevocable, with pain, loss of function, humiliation, dependency and then death, how would we then argue of suicide? The problem may not be major, for most sick people do not self-destruct in an open obvious act. For those few who might be driven to control their dying in this manner, why would we plead otherwise? Would we and should we, offer false promise, false hope, false futures just to allow a slow, disintegrating death at a slightly later date? I am not preaching in favor of suicide and as indicated, the number of suicides secondary to a discovered fatal illness is small. But would we always insist that suicide is evil?

There is still a considerable argument in medical writings as to whether the physician should or should not tell a patient that he has cancer, especially if the disease is not curable. There are always anecdotes of an individual, who upon learning the truth, goes into a deep depression, causing the physician regret that the truth came out. Just as often, there are warnings about the patient who does not want to know, and therefore should not be told. There are further tales of persons, especially physicians, who should certainly know better, denying that they have cancer after being told, and acting as if they had a mild, benign disease.

The trouble with all such anecdotes is that there is a tendency to exploit them into principles which then govern all subsequent relationships. The question is not what some, or even many, persons might do with information, but the basic right of an individual to openly participate in his life, fatally directed as it may be by illness. If a person's life is really his, if it really belongs to him, then the first essential question is his right to the truth about himself. If such expressions as courage, will, love and dignity are to have meaning, they must be allowed and encouraged to exist. This, I believe, applies to all stages of a fatal disease as an individual will significantly alter how he can confront and cope with the excruciating dilemma of fatalness and of his living unto death.

In a functional sense, how the diagnostic information of a fatal illness is imparted to a person, by whom and in what context, are exquisitely important to the functions of that person and to the function of people in his environment. Each person is an individual and requires individual understanding. There certainly are those who caution the physician that they do not want to know *bad news* and will make it clear that they do not care what is done as long as they do not have to know about it. Such individuals may have used denial patterns to all of life's vicissitudes and trials, and are extending this personality trait to this latest and potentially most awesome of personal confrontations.

Such psychologic defenses should be respected, but one must be sure that they exist before respecting them. All too often, information is withheld in the name of denial, but the denial may be in the physician or in the family, and not in the patient. Although time consuming, it is also important to attempt to learn why that person does not want to know. A previous experience with cancer in a loved one, a fearful and repressed image of dissolution or pain, an unresolved tension in some other life sphere may be causes for a person to flee from a confrontation with fatalness. Unless these defenses against confrontation can be explored, they certainly should be respected, if they exist.

How information is imparted, who does the telling and in what context, are critical. The more an individual physician knows his patient, knows the intellectual strengths, the religious convictions, the previous ways of handling crises, the previous emotional problems, the feelings for his family, the support likely from the family, the nature of his ambitions, then the better prepared he, the doctor, will be to impart information. The more that is known of the patient through knowledge of how often the patient has confronted cancer or death in loved ones before, by knowing what has been feared, what has been pleasurable, what has been meaningful, all these become guidelines as to how information is to be imparted and what to expect in symbolic and identity interpretations.[11]

Ideally, information regarding a patient's condition should be delivered gently, tactfully and progressively. Timing is critically important, and even the first communicative contact should be done when a person is alert and not groggy from anesthesia or drugs. Information should be delivered when the physician has time to sit quietly, unavailable to anyone but the patient, and unpressed to go running off to other chores. Not all information should be imparted initially, but enough implication of the meaning should be given so that the person may begin to absorb what is being said. Amplification of details can usually proceed gently in subsequent visits.

Unless it is completely certain that nothing in the way of treatment can be offered, the positive features of oncoming treatments should be elaborated, couched in terms of possible help and not absolute help. The door of potential therapy failure should always be left open. The hope residing in the subsequent treatments is of the greatest importance to a patient, but that hope must not be perverted into a promise of absolute cure. Hope must be regarded as a promise of possibility, not as an actuality. Absolute promises that are unfilled or unfillable, deny the chance for a future hope when it may be necessary for the individual to be so secured.

It is exceedingly important for family members to share in these communications and planning with the patient. Frequently, a physician burdened with his own perception of the truth and incapable of sharing this with a patient for fear of devastating that individual, will blurt out catastrophic news to a next of kin, intent on sharing this burden with a family member. Frequently such a tactic results in disarray in family relationships. Games that are played in attempts at protection lead to suspicions, dishonest tones, and frequently result in withdrawal from, and inability to face, the sick one. It is often better for all members of the family to be consonant and together, even if information is withheld from both patient and loved ones, rather than jeopardize mutual honest reapprochement.

If a person has a right to know of himself, in diagnostic and therapeutic terms, does he not also have the right to participate in what decisions are to be made for him? He will not be in authority and will have to lean heavily on advice offered professionally. But should he not have the right to an equal voice in decision making? Participating in decisions is not the same as simply accepting a decision. Few patients are boldly able to say 'no' when a major decision is given to them.

About four years ago I was asked to see a young lady, 24 years of age, because of a metastatic sarcoma of the leg. She had broken her leg in a minor fall and when hospitalized her chest X-ray revealed many cancer nodules. A biopsy revealed that the cancer had initiated in her leg. Her life expectancy was not particularly long and it was decided to treat her with new, chemotherapeutic drugs. But Eileen was two months pregnant. One of the side effects of the chemotherapeutic agents was potential damage to a young fetus and we, her physicians, knew of her short, expected survival. She was therefore strongly urged to undergo an abortion, stressing that the chemotherapy was necessary, and the danger to the fetus required termination of the pregnancy. We did not openly discuss the extent of the illness, its potential for her demise, or the limitations in her treatment for real improvement. Eileen underwent the abortion.

Months later, when her illness had progressed and she was closer to death, and after we had shared many hours discussing the meaning of her willness and of her life, she angrily discussed that abortion. She felt that she had not been presented with the truth of her condition, nor with the full facts of how limited in expectation the drug treatments were. Therefore, she had not been permitted to make a choice as to whether she wanted to keep the pregnancy. Could we not have openly discussed the full meaning of her illness in a manner that would have allowed her to participate in decisions about herself? This issue was not raised at the time that the medical staff concurred with the need for the abortion. Eileen may or may not have responded differently had we been able to spell out matters clearly. Regardless of any psychiatric implications, I now believe that she had the right to know what we knew and not to be deprived of information. Nor do I think we can say that if a patient truly wants to know, that he will ask. The truth of oneself is fearful, and asking requires a sense of personal strength and a trusting relationship. The absence of such conditions inhibits asking, but does not mean that the individual does not suffer from doubts and uncertainties.

We could conclude that Eileen was angry at not getting better and was unleashing her hostility, not about the pregnancy, but about the failure to improve. If the drugs had improved her condition, would that have made her grateful months later, rather than angry?

I asked that last question of Eileen and received the following reply:

> "Of course if I had been cured or improved for a long length of time, I would have accepted the abortion, for then I might have been able to have more children. But if there was little chance of that cure happening, shouldn't I have known that? And being so overwhelmed by the illness initially, I could not say 'no' to what you wanted to do!"

A fatal illness can induce "victimization" by the concentration of medical efforts into biologic care at the expense of emphathetic, supportive, esteem-directed care. The institutionalization of health care, the growth of specialty centers and the development of professional specializations has markedly delimited the meaning of fatal disease into disease terms and not human terms. In a busy, impersonal institution, who is to take the time to get to know the psychologic and social perspective of that sick person before communicating information to him? Who is to come to know how he symbolizes his life, his ambitions, his failings, his illness? Who is to help in allowing courage and self-control to emerge.

Ideally, the astute, well-trained physician should be that individual —advocate as well as technician, psychologist as well as physician, counsellor as well as operator, intuitive as well as organized. But this is not commonly true today, excused by the vast array of biologic data requiring concentration on the disease process itself. Extremely limited time in the educational format in the medical school, and too often in the college, does not allow for in-depth exploration of the meaning and ideals of men and their societies. Once the young medical student or physician enters into clinical duties in the hospitals, the elaboration of *doing* skills concentrates on the short-time exposure to the illness and the sick person. Intense energies are channeled into the healing of disease. This orientation, with its limited exposure to the sick, is a good working model in acute, shortlived illness, requiring intense and rapidly mobilized skills. There is great need to continue training physicians to function in such a model.

Another design is needed, however, in both fatal and chronic illness, for it is now, that a "futureless" or "future-limited" goal impresses itself onto medical procedures. The human patient needs something more than the rapid-restitution model, and the physician and the institution seldom seem educated to understand or to participate in such need. Perhaps the physician or the institution could be so trained, perhaps not. Perhaps it is too threatening to a physician's ego to live with *losing,* as long as we characterize dying as losing. But if the physician can't be so trained, then the institution must be changed.

Perhaps we should not try to disengage the future physician from his life-oriented, cure-structured primary role. Perhaps all of his energies should be so directed. What may be needed then, is another, or others, in the clinical world, who can deal with the issues of meaning, communication and support for the patient. These others would be professionals (since our world is composed of professional-client helping systems) whose specific training and function would be directed toward achieving a *good* living and a *good* death for the patient, and a moving towards resolution for the family. Trained to appreciate psychology, sociology, family-function, religion, the arts, these individuals could also be trained to the pharmacology of pain medications, tranquillizers and similar drugs. The roles of these persons would not be to conflict or antagonize the patient-physician relationship, but to greatly amplify what is being offered to the patient and his family, and to help the latter openly participate in decision making and in staying in control of limited options.

I have brought the family into the problem for the most obvious of reasons, yet they are characteristically exempted from a conception of their own needs in the typical working of a modern hospital. It is not that physicians, nurses and social workers are impervious to the suffering in a family group as fatal and terminal illness affects a loved member of the family, and that kindness and concern is not expressed for them. It is that such expression is given in terms of the patient and his progress and seldom in terms of the trauma within each family member, and the symbolic interpretation of the illness in their own, singular, unique terms. I will return to this later, but for now, it is important to recognize that family members suffer in their personal, psychologic ways. With the loss of the family doctor who supposedly knew the family in the home setting and tended to their needs, and with the growth of institutional disease-oriented caregiving, the needs of family members have been overshadowed by the operational tasks around the patient.

Who can this fatal illness caretaker be? If we lived in a single ethnic-cultural-religious environment, he could be a well-trained clergyman. During a recent trip to Ireland and Spain in which I tried to learn how the dying were looked after in different cultures, in response to my question about psychology, I was informed that the priest was the psychologist. This response was less emphatic in Dublin and Madrid, where modern worldly movements have considerably diminished the influence of the Church. In our pluralistic, polyglot society, modern and secular, a priest or minister could seldom be the only psychologist, yet the comforts of religion do exist for many, and where appropriate, should be utilized to the maximum. Clergymen are becoming psychologists in the present academic sense and frequently wish to function as a compliment to the psychiatrist on psychology's terms as well as religion's. The clergy have more than a passing role in illness, dying and counselling, and should be made a member of any group of *others* struggling towards euthanasia.

Probably the most significant other would be a nurse or a person with good nursing skills, trained in psychology, especially in the psychology of loss and in family counselling. A psychologist or social service worker could easily be trained to work in this area, but I believe that the direct management of pain, with the free ability to use medications, is vital to this role, and nurses might well be better at the total job. It would be foolish to believe that psychologists or social workers could not learn some nursing skills and I would hope that this could be done. It may, however, not be necessary, for there are several equally cogent tasks, and working with the family members as well as with the patient on many of the psychologic and social issues involved, is a task of a high order requiring many people with multiple skills and talents. A psychiatrist participating with these others, and certainly a well-trained physician, could complete a group, or a team, directing their composite energies towards helping a patient and his family, his doctors and his nurses.

The working of such a group, or a single member of that group, is toward a constructive "living in dignity," and euthanasia, and a help to families in mourning. While the physician is attempting to treat disease and to control symptoms as best as he can, support could be provided in his own struggles with making decisions in a manner that enhances rather than diminishes the patient's dignity and self-esteem, and creates a world of trust for that individual and his family—both trust in themselves as well as a trust for the outside world. A family that is open and supportive in helping a loved one to live with a fatal illness, can be a great asset in helping a person to die well. When open communication between a person and his family has developed, with secrecy and collusion avoided, great strength for all exists. Many families have difficulty in coping with open communication. Where patterns of response through the years have been denial or secrecy or unsharing, or in destructive reactions, support in the dying time can only be less than adequate. Not only does the patient pay a price for this inadequate support, but so do family members, both during the time of fatal illness and after death.

Fatal illness demands that the triad of patient, family and medical helpers must be seen as an interdependent group, each of whom needs support to sustain their individual self-images, their senses of trust and worth and their goals and interpretations of success or failure. In this present institutionalized world of illness and dying, a new scheme must be created for the structuring of such support. A team of people with appropriate skills aimed at a successful resolution of dying, is needed.

A support group of this nature, dependent for size and composition on the institution or environment in which it is to function, should have the two coordinates of time and space. Working with patients and families should begin early, at the time a fatal diagnosis is first made. Understanding the personality makeup of the individual patient and key family members should be an early support strategy. Patients with fatal illnesses have periods of time, highly variable, to live with their illnesses. In certain types of cancer this might be years, in other cases, merely months. People with chronic renal diseases may now live years, and certainly many heart disease patients and stroke patients live months to years.

During this living period, needs change as minimal symptoms of disease eventuate into greater debility. Dependency needs change, becoming greater as disease progresses. Each step in the process of a fatal illness requires a different dimension of support. What exactly will be required depends on the past history of the individual and on the history of his relationship with others. These others may also have problems in relating to the patient and often require some support on their own terms so that in effect, they can then offer support and encouragement to each other and to the patient. In the long and short run of time, it will be this intra-group support for each other, for the patient and for the physician, that will determine the ultimate manner of living, dying and mourning.

A team of individuals, so organized, is not a substitute for the physician. He still remains a vital force in caretaking. But for the physician, the problem may more often than not be *possessiveness,* either from a lack of perspective or the concern for self-image. The physician may frequently prevent existing ancillary services in an institution, such as social workers, from entering into a relationship with the family or patient, unless some specific issue arises. It is not always apparent why willing workers are kept out of helping roles except that frequently the medical problem is innocently defined only in its disease terms, and the enormity of the psychologic and social burden is just not recognized. Again, the physician may truly feel that controlling the illness is the most humanitarian action, and he is already devoting maximum energy to just that activity. Physicians who feel this way may not be protecting themselves from other professionals or possessing the patient for any exclusive need.

Physicians can speak of psychology in the abstract, but define the term operationally in "kindness" terms or fatherly terms. Death is an easy topic to discuss in the asbtract, but dying is yet all too often seen as a physician's failure. Since failures can be difficult to confront, avoidance of the possibility of death in a fatal illness, or avoidance of the fatal illness itself by name or by implication, may be a way of protecting the patient, the family and the physician himself. It is as if we could avoid the impact of a problem by refusing to deal with it. Thus, the physician or the family may twist the word "cancer" into tumor or mass, or a number of other names.

These disguises aim to protect the patient, the family and the medical staff from confronting the issue of fatality. Physicians who are in need for this protection for patients, or for themselves, may look upon a team of supporting professionals as intruders, as threats, or as nosy bodies. They might well be termed "unneeded" and excluded from utilization. It may take an exceptional bit of salesmanship to convince the physician, and the institution, that such help in working through the problems of patient and family is critically needed.

As indicated, all too often there is the wish to protect a person from knowing the essential truth about his threatened state of affairs. The physician may inform one or more family members of the facts and interpretations of a diagnosis, but keep this knowledge from the patient, offering instead, a more innocent interpretation of the illness, or a totally misleading one. The family may be instructed to keep the truth from the patient, again to protect against reactions of depression, anxiety or possible suicidal thoughts or actions. Sometimes it is the family that may insist, upon learning the diagnosis and prognosis, that the medical staff keep this information from the sick individual. In either case, or in cases of doubt and argument within a family as to the proper action, secrecy or collusion are immediately cast and the seeds of disruption rather than support emerge.

There simply is no way, in this frail biologic condition called life, to avoid pain and suffering. Attempts at protecting a person from truth may relieve the hurt of an immediate reaction, but must inevitably fail as an individual weakens and worsens with time. Disguising reality frequently forces a person to the added depression of lonely suffering. Sharing pain does not necessarily eliminate it but certainly brings consolation and bearability.

Simply allowing or encouraging people to share their thoughts or feelings, to *ventilate*, helps enormously. Often, this is all that can be done.

The purpose of a support group cannot be to eliminate suffering, eliminate death or eliminate the terrible sense of loss and grief. Help is to be seen as assisting the suffering to review their status, to reflect and find positive meanings in their present and past lives, to maintain close relations with loved ones needing them, to overcome feelings of isolation and abandonment, and to feel free to use these professional intermediaries to regain some sense of control over their lives. On a deeper level, help can be given to understand the anger that so frequently is present, but often distorted or displaced onto an innocent person or item when disease, or actual and threatened loss, exists. Feelings of guilt can be shared, and a better hold on reality established. Premature withdrawal of family, so frequent in long-term illness, can be helped, as well as guidance offered as to how a family can be of maximum help to the patient, the staff and to each other.

Death is too enormous an event for most people to stare at relentlessly. Hope for a future must always be allowable and encouraged. But hope does not imply delusion or deception. "Of course you'll get better" is not hope, but empty rhetoric, quickly reduced to empty words when time demonstrates impossibility. Hope itself is a changing dimension. Early in a fatal illness, hope implies that treatments might eradicate the illness, or more likely, postpone dying for a while. As an illness deepens, hope may be for pain-free days, the ability to enjoy an occasional good meal, getting out once in a while, looking for tomorrow rather than next week. But hope is best operative when magic and fantasy are shaved away and support and mutual togetherness exists.

In the story of a single man's particular confrontation with death, Lael Wertenberger describes her husband's meaning of trust as follows: "To be deceived about the nature of the progress of serious illness, or even to suspect deceit, would go far in destroying whatever fortitude one could summon to face one's trials."[12] Deception by one's physician or nurse or minister is hard enough to tolerate; deception by one's family can only result in furthered feeling of worthlessness and abandonment.

Perhaps this is not really such a terrible problem in closely-loved people, for planned deception tends not to work, although a knowing protection of one for the other, usually the patient for the other, emerges oftentimes. Fatally ill persons most often come to recognize the fatalness of their bodies through the body itself and through the actions of others. It is hard to effectively deceive a person when improvement is absent, or temporary, and when everyone around is behaving differently than expected. People learn intuitively from themselves, and implicitly from the actions and silent communications of others. Facing one's illness and one's dying is a trial and does take courage. The sick one may want to protect his loved ones from this awareness of his dying, but this consideration may be exhausting to him. His loved ones may try to protect him from their knowledge, but this too, proves exhausting frequently. Open communication does not mean that mutual hoping is abandoned. It really means that the worst moments, when they are there, can be shared, and that time for mutual planning for the future that will no longer contain the ill one, can be experienced.

Frequently, when all is in the open and mutual support exists, little further has to be said about dying. One can give so much more to living when play acting is not needed.

Just as necessary (in this work of living near dissolution and death continually) is an internal support for professionals, as well as the physician. We are so accustomed to thinking of death as failure, that even the most motivated of personnel must retreat from too much exposure. It may take a long, long time for the professionals to accept the fact that working towards a good death is rewarding and that it is professionally fulfilling to find support in one another, especially in the sharing of burdens and pains brought to the surface as so often happens when dealing with human suffering. Professionals identify with other humans and their heartaches easily, and threats to one's own sanity may exist in every encounter with human anguish. There is nothing easy in working with a dying patient or his family, and the lonely professional must retreat from the emotional intensity, or otherwise elect not to get involved. It is easy to insist that it is disease and not the human that is at stake, and that the real problem is biology. Much support is needed by the professional, be he physician, nurse, minister, technician or other, if effective help is to be forthcoming from him to deal with human suffering.

The functioning nature of institutions such as hospitals, and personnel within these institutions, needs to be examined. Institutions have a way of taking control away from patients in a manner most injurious to dignity, but consonant with institutional definition of efficiency. The incident cited earlier, that of keeping children out of the hospital, is an example of control at the expense of personal dignity. A dying patient or grandparent may well want, even need, to say a final goodbye to a young child. To deny that privilege is to take away a meaningful part of the dying experience. The kiss of goodbye, the touching and sharing of last moments, are exquisitely important to both the dying and the living. For an institution to obstruct this because of an arbitrary age is degrading, and clearly takes a sense of control and worth away from the dying.

The same applies to pets. A dear, childless, friend of mine died recently in a small, lovely, private hospital in Boston. She had two great loves beyond her husband, namely a two-year-old niece and her seven-year-old dog. Both were denied to her during her last three weeks in the hospital. Both were smuggled in, but a nurse caught the smuggling of the baby, and outraged, yelled at all concerned. Fortunately, this occurred after a most happy visit.

One could go on and on examining institutional behavior, such as control of pain medication, control of eating times, limitations on family caregiving as interference with the nurse's role. All such actions tend to diminish a person's image of himself, foster dependence and regression, and depersonalize.

Should a person die at home? The question is too complicated to answer in a categorical "yes" or "no." Energies should be directed for securing those community services that would allow a person maximum home stay, and death at home, if the person and the family are comfortable with the decision. Too many services today are concentrated only in hospitals, and too few hospital-based doctors and nurses can leave the institution to follow a patient at home.

If the principle of continuity-for-trust is to be maintained, a patient and his family must be able to move between home and institution freely, with the same general supporting people there to look after them. Specialists can be called in whenever needed, and special resources of the hospital or institution used as required, but only on-going continuing support by identifiable and reliable people can safeguard trust and security, and prevent unnecessary regression and slippage of personality. Continuity is the essence in trust, and while institutional continuity may sometimes be effectively seen, usually only personal continuity is satisfactory.

Our hospitals, now more than ever the mainstay in caregiving (with fewer and fewer medical practitioners and resources available to homes) must find ways of creating wall-less teams to assure continuity of care in the home as well as the institution, in a manner that is economically reasonable and geographically sane. Existing community resources must be linked to hospital resources in a fashion of ongoingness and must overlap so that discontinuity is not the rule. As such helping flowers, the question of home dying or hospital dying may cease to be the problem of today. People need help in dying, at home or otherwise, and if substantial help is not forthcoming at home, the institution must do.

Obviously a person's life is his in his home and it is here that he can feel in control of himself to the maximum. He may be driven out of the home by inadequate resources to keep him there, including family fears or exhaustion, or financial exhaustion, for most third-party insurance plans will not pay for home care. This is often only an indication of an unsatisfactory answer to absent effective home care strategies where money, courage or strength has been allowed to be sapped because of ineffective national medical planning. Families will frequently force loved ones into institutions, or the patient may elect the hospital or nursing home, rather than home itself, because of the threat of, or inability to, cope with a threatening physical problem when it arises, or because the fear exists that a hospital bed might not be available if needed immediately. Patients often do feel that they are burdens, and refuse to be at home out of deep consideration for their loved ones.

An effective home care program might well eliminate such considerations. Certainly economics is critical, and any home based program must provide support at a reasonable cost. Hospital or institutional care will always be needed for those alone with neither family nor friends to help, and for the many who simply cannot die or be allowed to die at home in this twentieth century, because the need to be looked after in a protective hospital environment has become too great. Needless to say, there are many, especially the elderly, with severe brain damage from senility or cerebral arteriosclerosis, who have ceased to be cognitive humans with inter-human potential. For these socially diminished or dead, to wait for biologic death at home is probably senseless and institutional care is vastly to be preferred.

We should be careful before assigning too many to that category. Providing economically sound, medically effective home care is a

clear reversal of our present strategies. To make such care part of
hospital function seems most difficult now, what with the present
hospital image as a complicated, technologic instrument for health
through cure. Yet where home care programs have been tried, the
results in human terms, have seemed considerable.[13] The pressure
for their expansion has been minimal, however, as the vociferous cry
of technology, proficiency and organization has centralized functions
within the institutions. It would take a national policy to bring about
change.

Can a team of professionals provide enough support to truly sustain
a person's dignity at the end phase of his life? Can enough self-control
be secured, enough family support developed, enough self-esteem and
self-fulfillment encouraged, that a man could truly die with tranquility? The answer may not be "yes" for all men. Too many have
lived lives of quiet desperation to find a peace at the end. The proposed team comes into the life late in its cycle and enough time may
not be available to resolve life's previous divisiveness, nor to help in-
still harmony where only anxiety exists. However, many a patient
has found acceptance and peace in dying and enough anecdotes exist
to convince that a peaceful disengagement from life, for the dying
and for his family, can occur more often than at present. Clearly,
new forms of research are necessary to aid in dying.

One line of research today is into the use of psychedelic drugs such
as lysergic acid diethylamide (LSD). Used in different ways, different results have been reported. A group of researchers in Baltimore,
using LSD together with many hours of psychotherapeutic preparation of the patient for the trip, report most encouraging outcomes,
especially if the patient has experienced the psychedelic *peak,* a transcendental point where the feeling of union with the cosmic in a joyous fulfillment is reached. It is not appropriate here to go deeply into
these qualities of a *good* trip and certainly this manner of use of LSD
is not an endorsement of home or street trafficking in the drug. A
carefully prepared and supervised LSD experience bears absolutely no
relationship to the potentially dangerous, popular use and abuse of
this drug. If the reports are to be believed, and prove to be repro-
ducible, the further exploration of LSD or other psychedelic agents as
a help to the dying, should continue. The reports are most impressive;

pain diminishes and becomes easily bearable, communication with family is reestablished, harmony and tranquility replaces anguish and withdrawal, and the fear of death decreases sharply.[14]

Many other agents, of different types, may be helpful, and exploration of these drugs should be mandatory. In England, heroin is used medicinally while such use is prohibited in the United States. Adherents of heroin claim that it brings a peacefulness, while relieving pain and anxiety, that other opiates cannot. Carefully performed drug trials have not been performed, to my knowledge, in England, but there certainly is no reason why such trials and use cannot be investigated in the United States. To be concerned about addiction in the dying process seems bizarre, and to be concerned that the legitimate presence of heroin would tempt and contaminate the innocent is to play ostrich to puritanic madness.

Another strategy worthy of consideration is the creation of new types of institutions for the fatally ill, especially for the dying. An example is the hospice idea, a place of refuge and safe passage, as opposed to a hospital. An extraordinary model has been in existence in London, England for some time, at St. Christopher's Hospice.[15] Established by Dr. Cecily Saunders, the hospice is located in a residential section of the city, away from the hubbub of downtown London, in an area of trees, gardens and quiet. Large, open wards allow an easy feeling of sharing and communion, but little flower-boxed corners make for personal niches of privacy. Light comes pouring in from large windows and an easy access to a spacious garden allows for the out-of-doors to be part of hospice routine.

Families are invited to share in the caretaking, and children and pets are as welcomed as adults. Nurses are expected to sit on beds and to be close with patients. Drugs such as heroin are freely used and gin is a standard part of hospice pharmaceuticals. Techniques are employed to avoid both actual and anticipated pain, and regular around-the-clock medication is used to keep patients free of the expectation of pain. Through it all is a feeling of doing an elite job of helping patients to die comfortably, at ease, and to offer families the solace of safe-keeping of their loved ones. Should a patient need technical hospital care, consultants are available, or transfer is possible. Generally, however, patients are admitted at the end of an illness, frequently cancer, when the regular hospitals feel that there is "nothing left to do." The hospice demonstrates how much can be done at that point.

The hospice is not home, but is so much closer to home than a large hospital. The hospice idea is one that might well benefit many dying patients needing a protective environment other than home.

[1]*The Living Will*. Obtainable from the Euthanasia Educational Fund, 250 West 57th Street, New York, N.Y. 10019.

[2]Bacon, Francis: *The Advancement of Learning and New Atlantis*. London, Oxford Press, 1956, p. 133.

[3a]Marx, Karl F.H.: Medical Euthanasia. A paper reintroduced by Walter Cane. *Journal of the History of Medicine and Allied Sciences*. 7:401-416, 1952.

[3b]Rohlfe, Gottfried H.: *Geschicter der Deutschen Medizin*. Stuttgart, Enke, 1880.

[4]Frankl, Viktor E.: *The Doctor and the Soul*. New York, Alfred A. Knopf, 1955.

[5]Kubler-Ross, Elizabeth: *On Death and Dying*. New York, MacMillan, 1969.

[6]Weisman, Avery: *On Dying and Denying*. New York, Behavioral Publications, 1972.

[7a]Hinton, John: *Dying*. Baltimore, Penguin Books, 1967.

[7b]Quint, Jeanne C.: *Nurse and the Dying Patient*. New York, MacMillan, 1967.

[8]Frankl, Viktor E.: *Man's Search for Meaning: An Introduction to Logotherapy*. New York, Washington Square Press, 1963.

[9]Notes of a dying professor. *Pennsylvania Gazette*, March, 1972, pp. 18-24.

[10]Currier, Lawrence M.: The psychological impact of cancer on the cancer patient and his family. *Rocky Mountain Medical Journal*, February, 1966.

[11]Verwoerdt, Adriaan: *Communication with the Fatally Ill*. Springfield, Ill. Charles C Thomas, 1966.

[12]Wertenbaker, Lael Tucker: *Death of a Man*. New York, Random House, 1957.

[13]Pfeiffer, Mildred C.J., and Lemon, Eloise M.: A pilot study in the home care of terminal cancer patients. *American Journal of Public Health and the Nation's Health*, 43:909-914, 1953.

[14]Pahnke, Walter N., Kurland, Albert A., Unger, Sanford, Savage, Charles, and Grof, Stanislav: The experimental use of psychedelic psychotherapy. *Journal of the American Medical Association*, 212:1856-1863, 1970.

[15]Saunders, Cecily: *A Therapeutic Community: St. Christopher's Hospice in Psycho Social Aspects of Terminal Care*. B. Schoenberg, A.C. Carr, D. Peretz, A.H. Kutcher (Eds.). New York, Columbia University Press, 1972.

CHAPTER VI

FAMILIES OF THE DYING

I WOULD LIKE to elaborate further about families, their problems, perceptions and interactions in regard to fatal illness and the dying of a loved one. The definition of the term "family" has changed considerably in the past years, and I do not intend to abide in the danger of concentrating on one standard social arrangement to the diminishing of other important interpersonal ties. However, what I have to say about families should be allowable to any individual inter-related to another in a long lasting history, be he or she friend, lover or ex-mate.

When one speaks of death and dying in a family context, two images can usually be envisioned, both blended into the one person. There is the role that the dying person plays in the family, as well as the personal meaning of that individual to another family member. A dying father may be bread winner, car driver, house fixer, toy repairer, punishment giver, etc., but he may also be an object loved for his personal sake, hated for his personal traits or alternately loved and hated, sequentially or simultaneously. He may be a person little more than someone whose roles can be replaced by another, or he can be critical in love-hate relationships and irreplaceable as such. The meaning of dying and death can best be understood if we can see that the loss of an important family member threatens certain social arrangements in which the dying member plays an important role, as well as interpersonal psychologic dependency relations inherent in the terms love and hate.

Much has been written about families in crises, and there has been a spate of recent publications accusing the family structure of being an enemy to individual happiness. The western family is certainly a family of intense dependencies, and the growth of small nuclear units has probably served to heighten the dependency tendencies. Perhaps in its best form, a small nuclear family with its members concentrating their effect on each other, allows maximum loving to emerge and promotes deep feelings of importance, if not omnipotence, in the few involved. On the other hand, deep dependency also creates anger and hostility at the dependent relationship, especially for children growing into adolescence.

With the acceptance that an early separation from the parental home is part of life, either in the form of going off to college or to an out-of-town job, or to early marriage, middle-aged people are left rather early in life to their own devices, and to each other. Dependence on each other becomes maximized, both for social role and for personal support. Sometimes such face-to-face confrontation of "only us two" may result in breaking up a marriage either by divorce or by establishing more intense separate out-of-home activities. Or, two middle-aged parents may find the freedom to enjoy things together for the first time in a long time.

Fatal illness in a family, especially if it occurs to one of the now-alone middle-aged or elderly adults, or in a live-alone adult separated from spouse and children, creates enormous stresses in all the various members of the family. Sudden death, of course, in one of such a duo, creates immediate problems for the surviving spouse, and the children living apart, in terms of life-style and interpersonal dependency. Although the problems arise acutely in some ways, the issue is a clear one, though intensely painful.

Resolution of grief in this latter circumstance may be difficult enough, and self-blame and guilt may be intense in the survivor. A fatal illness carries another burden, in some ways heavier, in the need to participate in the dying process, and the continuous pain and threat implied in such awareness. Since, in the modern world, there is little style or acceptable place for dying itself, and little direction as to what constitutes a "good" dying for the ill individual, there is frequently a misunderstanding of how to help a sick loved one to live with a fatal illness, and to die peacefully. The terms dignity, self-esteem, control, support, trust, love and self-fulfillment may not be the most commonly sought after goals in marriage and child rearing, and are difficult goals to bring about in the dying process, not just for an individual dying, but for the interrelating family members as well.

Perhaps this can best be understood if we attempt an analysis, weak though it may be, of what it is that constitutes dependency relationships. Mature love relationships can perhaps be characterized by a positive leaning towards the other who is seen to possess virtues, strengths, concepts, abilities, characteristics and appearances that can be called beauty, goodness, warmth, truth and trust. The existence of such characteristics in a loved one allows the loving one to feel a beauty, truth, trust and goodness in himself in relation to the positive identification of the other. The issue is really not taking something or demanding something from the other in order to gratify a personal sense of absence or shortcoming, but allowing for an ongoing growth and freedom in both partners independently, yet in close relation to the other.

Mature loving does not demand protection and safety from the other, but takes it for granted that such protection and safety exists in the accepting of the other for what he or she is. Mature love allows independent function of the other, an encouragement for continued growth and change, and a sense of peace and harmony through the nature of the relationship which exists. One can feel joyous and peaceful without demanding that the other give up his or her own specific identity to meet unfulfilled needs. At the same time, loving implies bonding, or attachment, and it is this bonding to another, that feeling of belonging and needing the belonging, that is so much a part of loving.

When such a relationship exists between a man and a woman, between parents and children, and between brothers and sisters, one is constantly on the alert to support the dignity and esteem of the other and feels right in doing so. When such relationship does not exist, the concern for the other's dignity and esteem is secondary to the use of the other to supply needs to make the loving one feel adequate or purposeful. Maturely loving people spend time, just as do less mature people, wondering about money, eating, housing, vacations, schooling and the like, but they seem to be freer in accepting these worldly routines in the context of mutuality and respect for the other.

Just as the dying time can be prolonged for a person fatally ill, with no guarantee that good living time will be automatically included in the dying days, that same time can be rewarding or exhausting, fulfilling or empty, uniting or divisive, growing or regressive, loving or hating, for family members. The quality of that time will be clearly related to the meaning of the fatally ill person in the family in the past, as well as in the present. Where there has always been a deep regard for the other, a meaningful relationship based on deep-seated mutual affection and support, then a continued support and encouragement for living is often seen in the mutual experience of dying and losing. When there has been little personal affection and regard, there is apt to be much anger and fear on the part of family members, or even a sense of relief at the freedom that death will bring.

Truly supportive, loving, intimate relations occur often enough, yet there would appear to be a rather high percentage of families where collusion and scapegoating exists, or where ambivalent relations are common. When a fatal illness develops in such a family, members become engaged in protecting themselves, or hurting others, rather than openly supporting each other. Perhaps better stated, there frequently develops an ambivalent position in regard to support and self-protection. The mixed, ambivalent feelings may not be present in the early days of a fatal illness when all energies are exerted to find appropriate help through medical diagnosis and treatment to cure or forestall the condition.

But as a disease process, such as cancer, drags on and on, and quick and easy solutions to the many problems emerging do not appear, strain and stresses are placed on family members that can promote exhaustion, impatience, anger and a sense of futility. The sense of duty and obligation frequently weakens and various members begin to withdraw from the patient, claiming that there are legitimate pressing needs of their own, such as business, their own nuclear families or school. Consequently, fewer and fewer people become available for continued duty and support. Such physical withdrawal compounds the chores and responsibilities physically and psychically, for the few who are duty bound to continue support week after week.

The emotional nonsupport, the feeling of abandonment for both the patient and his remaining kin, is most difficult to take. The loneliness so often described in dying is brutally emphasized in such self-protecting withdrawing. When only two adult members of a nuclear family are together, the children off in their own personal nuclear worlds, brothers and sisters busy with their defined lives and parents no longer alive or too old to really help, the physical and emotional strain on the healthier one can be enormous, and the resultant anger at the world intense. Shock, anger and depression coexist for short or long periods of time when the full awareness of a progressively fatal illness develops. These feelings occur in patients, but they also appear in dependent family members.

The many difficult medical treatments that attempt to cure, forestall or palliate frightening complaints, especially in the cancer field, result in disfigurement and body alteration, and are often as difficult for the family to accept as they are for the patient. If a person has a long future after such treatment, effort can be expanded in rehabilitation, psychologically and physically. But if the illness results in decline, despite the treatments, little time and effort is available to rehabilitate the patient, especially psychologically, and even less time is available for the family. As the patient incurs the loss of feelings of selfness, of esteem and of worthiness, which may lead to depression, to anger, to a sense of futility, family members frequently share in such feelings.

As sickness worsens and physical debility increases, complaints may quicken. Hostility generated from helplessness and futility with life's conditions, can cause a patient to lash out at family member nearby. Meals are complained about, the temperature in the house is wrong, the newspaper is wrinkled and on and on. Anger can become intermixed with fear and clinging. Complaints such as pain, headache, nausea, shortness of breath, sleeplessness, restlessness, irritability, become ways of expressing such an effect. Hostile lashing out may be the result of jealousy for the healthy, of futility with unfulfilled ambition, or of deep feelings of worthlessness. Those around such a patient may be driven to exhaustion trying to please an unrelenting, demanding, angry sick one. Family members may feel guilty for taking a walk, going for a drive, doing anything at all for themselves, for the patient appears never to be pleased and ordinary events of living come to be seen as betrayals.

Given this pattern of behavior, care at home, even care in the in-

stitution, becomes difficult to impossible. A family may be forced
to seek hospitalization for a loved one and then have trouble with
feelings of guilt and corresponding anger. Such emotional reactions
can lead to projected anger against caretakers, with fault being found
with hospitals, doctors, nurses as well as with brothers, sisters, uncles,
etc. When faced with a declining family member, especially a dying
family member, many people feel an obligation to give up all pleasurable pursuits in order to placate a feeling of seriousness, including
feelings of guilt, and the sense of obligation not to appear light-hearted
or frivolous.

Many people take this obligation to heart, to maintain the stance of
seriousness. Trips are cancelled, theatre and movies are suspended,
dinners with friends are unthinkable. If the sick individual is comatose, or close to death, the family may have every need to be near at
hand and withdrawn from other activities. However, if the fatally
ill decline gradually, with days, weeks or perhaps months before
death, it is of critical importance for involved family members to be
able to get away. Everyone needs to be renewed, to regain vigor
and strength, in order to continue in attendance. In a family where
only one person is "stuck" with caregiving and others have retreated,
the ability of that one involved person to get away becomes sharply
delimited, aggravating the hostile, martyr-like feelings already propa-
gated.

Depression is frequently found in the patient with terminal illness,
and this state amplifies an already difficult home or hospital situation.
Efforts at cheering up are invariably rejected, and a family may feel
that nothing they do makes any difference. Living with this helpless
feeling becomes painfully frustrating. Children try to please and
are pained for their efforts. Grandchildren are confused by a grandmother who used to laugh and play with them, but who now may
refuse even to acknowledge their presence, or may cry in front of
them that she'll never see them again. Parents may be confused
as to whether they should let their children see and be "abused"
by a depressed grandparent. Protecting children from seeing "bad
things" is so much a need for parents. If, in addition to depression,
grandmother smells badly, cannot move her left arm, is now gaunt
and frail or has a tube running into her nose and down to her stomach,
parents feel obligated to shelter their children.

Long-term fatal illness is exhausting to all concerned. Besides the emotional problems, day-to-day chores can be overwhelming, especially if they involve actual nursing care of the sick. If there is much physical suffering or much physical wasting, it is painful for a family to witness; painful not only for what one can see, but for the humiliations that the body seems to be heaping on the spirit and personality of the loved one. If open wounds exist, incontinence is present, foul smells emanate, a feeling of repugnance can drive one away from the sick person. That pain of being witness to such terrible changes can often lead one to wish for death and an end to the outrageous insult. "I don't see how he can stand it" is often projected onto the patient as an expression of a family member's own feelings. Even in the most loving of relationships, an impatience to see it all over can be sensed, not necessarily to get on with living, but because of the futility of another painful day.

If death is to be inevitable, it should not be dragged on, mercilessly and needlessly. Yet, what an impossible thought to entertain! At least living is here, dead is gone! Where ambivalence (as is so common) has existed in family relations, where love and hate, admiration and anger, mutual esteem and mutual distrust have lived side by side inside of people, wishing for a loved one to die and yet hoping for another day, may tear at the guts of a spouse or child.

Losing a loved person is painful. Losing someone loved and depended upon can be unbearable, for not only is the personality of the individual who is dying being lost, but the identifiable world of the survivor is in threat. The roles played by the dying person are disappearing, and the more dependent the survivor has been on these roles to define a position in the world, the more threatening death becomes. As death comes closer, the anguish of "what will I do now," or "what will I be now" presses closer and closer. These are selfish thoughts and cannot be easily verbalized as a spouse or sibling lies dying; attention must honorably be directed towards the patient.

However, this is not always possible. Frightened, angry families will often begin to compete for attention from others in the environment by developing their own complaints, or aggravating preexisting ones. These may frequently be symptoms similar to the ill and dying person's but not necessarily so. Often it is the gastrointestinal tract that becomes the focus, with aches, vomiting, nausea, bowel disturbances. It may well be in the musculo-skeletal system, with complaints in the joints, shoulders or arms. Headaches and dizzy spells are not uncommon. These complaints seem to be screaming that one should pay attention to the spouse, to the one who is losing, the one who must go on living. There is little room in such a reaction to be concerned for the dignity of dying.

Often, the only way of handling the dying of a needed one is to suppress and deny the thought of death. Such denial can place great strain on relationships in the family, especially if the person with a fatal illness is well aware of what is happening to him. The denying spouse or sibling often places great strain on the medical staff by insisting that matters are improving, or demanding that the patient be discharged shortly, when conditions hardly warrant such interpretation. A lack of "acceptance" (perhaps not quite the same as denial but close enough to it emotionally), may result in a family member insisting on many medical consultations, or even running off to charlatans or quacks who are always ready to take advantage of such disquiet. This is not meant to imply that there is only one way of treating the patient with fatal illness, and that patients and families do not have the right to seek whatever help they wish. Most people search for unproven and magical medical methods as a fantasy-rescue, rather than as a thought out, studied response. Frequently it is the family, hearing of some unproven treatment somewhere, or of some person who was deathly sick but now healthy after treatment, who insist that the patient try the treatment, even at the risk of mortgaging the home.

The terribly sad part of such behavior is that fraud or trickery is so often at the base of such treatment, causing economic and psychologic embarrassment for patient and family, and a flight into nonrescuing magic resulting in heightened despair. I know of no scientific evidence to support the following statement but would hypothesize that a fair amount of such flight is the result of ambivalent relationships between patient and family member, in which the acceptance of a fatal illness and dying is impossible due to either considerable unresolved anger and consequent guilt, or to overdependence in the family relationship. Certainly, fatal illness and death are not romantic illusions, and simply accepting terminality without fighting for life is not a mark of the loving of life. Legitimate fighting and fantasy rescuing are scarcely the same phenomenon, even though at times the line of distinction may not be obvious.

Perhaps the overly technical side of medicine, if little true compassion and communion exists between the suffering and the caretaker, results in enough distrust and absence of harmony, that flight to the charlatan, who frequently is quite stylistically empathetic, is encouraged.

For the family as well as for the patient, the issue is how to provide for a peaceful living, a tranquil death and a good mourning. By "good" mourning, I do not mean obliteration of pain, for this is inconceivable. To love and need someone means to suffer when that someone is lost. A sudden death puts the survivor into a sudden state of shock and disbelief which must then be followed by a gradual, painful, acceptance of the death. To be a participant in the slow dying from a fatal illness allows for beginning mourning before death occurs.

The key to the problem of continued and ongoing living, and the resolution of mourning, is the manner and meaning of the dying of the loved one. When a survivor feels a sense of ease with the dying process itself, recovery in mourning is facilitated. When there are unresolved feelings of guilt, blame or anger, then long lasting despair and a chronic, unresolved state of mourning can result.

This is not to imply that a peaceful death will result in the absence of deep feelings of loss, and that many social as well as psychological problems will be obviated. Such, unfortunately, is not the case. A long, intimate and mutually supportive marriage can result in deep loneliness and emptiness for the survivor no matter how acceptable and peaceful that death has been. Women who have been protected and sheltered by caring husbands, and who have identified their lives through the life activities of a mate, may find it difficult at best to get along in a strange, new role of widow, requiring new skills such as handling money, writing checks, driving a car, getting from place to place, going on a social call alone. There are few agencies or groups concerned with the manner of living for lonely widows and widowers, but there is some evidence that social programs such as widow-to-widow groups are developing, and that civic and church groups are attempting to organize to meet the needs of such lonely survivors.[1]

Greater problems await the family where conflicts and tensions developed or worsened during fatal illness. The unresolved psychologic strains of such conflicts can lead to severe psychiatric, physical and social diseases after death has occurred. A British psychiatrist, studying the patterns of grieving of women who required hospitalization in psychiatric institutions after the death of a loved one, and comparing these patterns to women who grieved but did not require such extensive psychiatric help, noted that guilt and self-blame were far more common and intense in the former than in the latter.[2] The hospitalized patients felt that they had not done enough for the dead, loved person, or that in some way, they were responsible for the illness or the outcome. Guilt of this nature may not be identified as justified by an objective observer. No obvious omission or faulty performance can be verified. But self-blame is the perception of wrong-doing, and is often related to anger and conflicts unresolved during the lifetime of the now deceased person.

As mentioned, serious psychiatric and physical illnesses have been seen to develop following a pathological grief reaction. By pathological, I mean a grief reaction that does not resolve itself in a period of time, say two to four months, although we are not certain as to the outer limits of normal grieving. (There is evidence that some aspects of "normal" grieving may persist beyond a year.)[3] A good grieving means essentially that the mourner experiences and participates in the many painful and sad reactions to the loss of a loved one and gradually begins to return to living in a meaningful way.

Good grieving does not imply that all memories or traces of the lost one are obliterated or forgotten; quite the opposite. When a person experiences good grief and works through the pain of the loss, memories and recollections persist in a warm, supportive fashion, creating the feeling of a good past. The dead loved one is tenderly remembered forever into the future, but the living are not enslaved to those memories in a fashion that prevents new and lovely social, sexual, intimate relationships from developing. The living can find pleasure in new relationships or marriage. Other love relationships can and do happen. Painful recollections may frequently appear even after a good grieving, especially around important times such as a birthday, an anniversary, a sudden awareness of a previously shared moment or event. On the whole, after a period of time, one can talk about, or think about, the lost loved one with warm rather than painful feelings.

Pathological grief is the absence of such resolution. The memory of the dead one always is painful and possessing, and new relationships may be impossible to make. Sometimes no real grieving is seen, and the mourner seems never to go through the pain of inwardly experiencing the loss. It is not the purpose of this book to document and discuss the ramifications of grief and bereavement, nor to discuss the social and cultural climate that has made open mourning socially out-dated, leaving the griever much on his own, unsupported by society at large.[4] I am simply stating that the nature of the dying itself may well have a long-range influence on the living as exacted in the bereavement process. Grief and bereavement are the common lot of all men, as is dying. One cannot live a social existence and not know loss. Grief may be a demand of life, but a prolonged and abnormal grief reaction is an unfortunate outcome. The manner of a loved one's dying and the behavior of the family during that time may be an instrumental factor in the recovery, or its absence, from grieving.

I have emphasized before the support to live that is possible for the dying, when the dignity and self-esteem of the ill individual is taken as a major objective by the professional staff and the family. I stressed that an open communication between all concerned, in which secrets were eliminated, protection of the other made unnecessary, mutual decision making for such things as hospitalization or home care, burial arrangements, wills, plans for the survivors after death, etc., were allowed, and loving good-byes encouraged, helped in the making of a dignified, peaceful death. The wishes of the dying can be known and complied with, resolution of previous antagonisms assisted, and an integrated meaning to life found. Sadness, weightiness, impending loneliness are present and not obliterated in such open communication. An open awareness and communication in the dying time can allow an expectant survivor to begin the mourning process. The meaning of the past life between the two individuals can be reviewed, good and warm memories explored, close and delightfully shared pleasure and intimacies relived. At the same time, the anticipated pain of living without the other can be allowed to emerge, the change in life roles and status can be openly considered and some planning for ongoing living can be begun. Allowing and encouraging such thought and pains may well free hidden fantasies, unresolved anguish and guilt. Forgiveness and blessings can be given. The particular resolution of conflicting thoughts between family members may allow a family as a whole to support the dying patient in a manner that brings a feeling of a job well done at a later time, rather than persistent guilt.

As important as attention to psychologic and interpersonal factors may be, families are often beset with physical problems of considerable magnitude in the long-term care of a fatally ill person. Many families are quite willing, if not anxious, to look after a loved one at home as long as possible. But as a sick individual becomes weaker and physical needs become greater, a burden clearly develops. Ill patients need to be fed, bathed, helped to be up where and when possible, or to be moved from bed to chair. Attention may have to be given to bowels, to sores, to swollen limbs, to pain and many other complaints. A family must often face the question of who is to give the attention required. If a man is working, who will look after his wife while he is away? Who will help mother look after the needs of her children if she must be caring for her parent, especially if he is in his own home a mile away? Who is to offer relief so that the principal caregiver can get out and away for a while?

If there are few members of the family available, or if those in the vicinity have their own needs to fulfill and wish to leave caretaking to only one person, how can it be managed? There exists a paucity of helping services in most communities, not just in visiting nurses, (whose presence is often an absolute must) but in housekeeping services, baby-sitting services and the like. What's more, the available services tend to be expensive, especially as time passes. Third party insurance will not cover most home expenses incurred, not even bandages.

Thus, home caring can be physically exhausting and financially draining. In addition, home caring is frightening, especially as physi-

cal complaints occur in patients. The lack of medical practitioners
for home visits creates a lonely and frightening position for family
and patient both. Supposing the patient dies at home? What is a
family to do? Who is to be called? Do they really want this to
happen?

A difficult physical care problem will often result in the family
seeking institutional care, either hospital, nursing home or extended
care facility for a patient, especially if elderly. The consequences of
such a decision for the patient are well known. The guilt and self-
blame for sensitive family members have also been recognized, but
frequently these problems are not attended to.

Long-term illness frequently engenders resentments resulting in
abandonment of the patient, and open or covert hostility between
various family members. People frequently find themselves trapped
into silences and secrets, either as a heritage of the past styles of living
together, or in an attempt to protect the patient, or each other, from
the pain of confronting the truth. Watching someone die may provoke
an intense and embarrassed feeling of helplessness. Frequently there
is conflict within the family as to what to do and what to say, not
only to the sick one, but to each other. There may well be a son who
cannot tolerate what he interprets as deceit, and who comes into direct
conflict with an aunt who insists that nothing about cancer or dying
be mentioned in the patient's presence. Anger, helplessness, and a
sense of futility flourish in such dissonance, causing further separation
and distance within the family.

Disinterested help is often needed. By disinterested, I do not mean
uncaring, but rather a nonfamily person trained in understanding
family tensions and needs in relationship to the fatal disease, one
who is trained to help in the struggle for harmony and togetherness.
Such a person is logically part of a treatment group working with
the patient and family, but also dedicated to seeing the problem
through the family's eyes and not the patient's or the system's alone.
Such helpers should be available in every hospital and community.

It should be stressed again that the most difficult problems facing
many families with a dying member are communication, support
and participation. Nothing will enhance confusion, anger, disappointment and mistrust more than the lack of open communication between

various family members, the patient and the medical staff. Patients may be forced into positions of protecting their families when they (the patients) suspect that they know the truth. But because the family is not discussing the obvious with them, they may feel that their spouses or children may not be aware of what is happening. I have seen many situations where new patients, coming into the hospital have confided to me that they know they have cancer and suspect that they will die shortly of the illness, but that I should not tell their families because it would so sadden them to know. Of course, when meeting the next-of-kin, exactly the reverse is revealed, namely, that they have been hiding the truth from the patient because he or she couldn't take it. "And please make sure that you don't tell him that he has cancer" comes as a request. The family always seems so startled to learn that the patient already knows, and has been trying to protect them just as the family has been trying to protect the patient.

Such protecting is not done easily. Not long ago a 68-year-old gentleman was referred to our medical unit with a diagnosis of advanced metastatic cancer. The disease had originated in an unknown site but had been diagnosed just three weeks prior to his admission to our unit, when a severe leg pain had brought him to the emergency room of a community hospital in one of Boston's peripheral towns. Destruction of the left femur was noted on X-ray and a biopsy revealed cancer. Further workup revealed that metastasis had already occurred to the liver and lungs. In retrospect, he had not been feeling well for some time, but nothing specific or overwhelming was wrong, and he had delayed seeking medical advice.

The patient's spouse was told, after the biopsy, that cancer had been found and that he did not have long to live. The diagnosis was kept from the patient, and instead he was told that he had an uncertain illness. When I asked his wife about the reasons for this decision, she was uncertain as to whether she had responded to the doctor's orders, or whether she and the physician had reasoned together that protecting her husband from this information was important. At any rate, by the time this couple came to our unit, it was obvious that they were both saddened and depressed. Each seeemed withdrawn into their own personal worlds. In speaking privately with Mr. M., he voluntarily confessed that for several reasons he thought he had a "bad" cancer, or something of that nature. He was suspicious of the way people were treating him, and was distressed that his wife had become so distant. We did not immediately confirm his suspicion but instead, spoke privately with his wife. She was quite nervous, fidgeting in the chair, left eye twitching, with her hands picking at the corner of a handkerchief. Yes, she thought that her husband knew something was seriously wrong and that he did not have long to live. How hard it was to be unable to share these moments with him. In 43 years of marriage they had shared everything, keeping nothing from each other. How difficult it was to have to play act and be in separate worlds at such a terribly important time for them. She further told us that she had been sleeping poorly, not only because she knew the seriousness of her husband's condition, but because she felt that she was cheating him, despite visiting him faithfully each day and remaining for long hours.

It was not hard to convince her that Mr. M knew the truth, that he wanted to protect her from having to confront the pain of that knowledge, and that they really needed each other more than ever at that point. We asked her permission to openly discuss the diagnosis and our course of treatment with both of them, and she quickly agreed. Returning to Mr. M's room, I simply asked him what he though was wrong with him. He stated again, but this time in his wife's presence, that he knew he had a serious cancer and might not have long to live. He said this looking softly at his wife, smiling faintly.

Little more had to be said. I mentioned something of the tests that we would do and some treatments available and left them together, holding hands. Mr. M. remained hospitalized for some weeks to receive irradiation treatments to the leg and physical therapy to help him transfer from bed to chair. Hope of various degrees of improvement and of sustaining comfortable life was offered both of them which they accepted gratefully and realistically. Both Mr. and Mrs. M. wanted to be at home, but he was concerned that she would not be able to care for him if he were totally bedridden and that he would be too much of a burden. Despite her insistence that she could do it, he wanted to protect her from injury in helping him, and he wished to be as self-sufficient as possible for as long as he could.

In recognizing his needs to avoid excessive dependency, his wife encouraged him to remain hospitalized a bit longer for his physiotherapy even though her own needs were to have him at home quickly. A number of medical approaches were discussed, including an operation to stabilize the leg further, and a course of chemotherapy. The pros and cons were discussed with them, especially the risks to be ventured for the potential gain. Risks such as prolonged hospitalization, further debilitation and the possibility of not returning home were all openly reviewed. It was decided that a short course of anti-cancer drugs were worthwhile but that surgery should not be attempted. Pain was easily controlled at this point with oral medications and Mr. M. was able to make the transfer to a chair with the use of his good leg and little weight bearing on his bad one. A hospital bed was arranged at home, and a physician-neighbor agreed to come in and look after him. Additional arrangements were made to have him return to our clinic by ambulance every three or four weeks. One of our nurses dropped in to see him at home.

Three children were involved in this story. The eldest daughter lived abroad with her husband and family and returned for a prolonged visit. The second daughter lived nearby with her family and visited regularly to support both parents. The most dramatic issue however, was their son, in his thirties and the M's youngest child. A university graduate, through the years he had become estranged from his wife, children, job, and parents and had resorted to heavy alcoholism. The M's had not seen their son for nearly a year prior to Mr. M's illness, although he lived in a neighboring suburb. Mrs. M. had notified him of his father's illness shortly after the original diagnosis was made and he had visited, but under instructions not to discuss the illness or its consequences. That one visit was the only one he found possible to make until his father called to tell him that he was aware of the nature of his illness and of his limited future. With communication open, the son returned to visit and both parents later informed me that he had stopped drinking, was back to work and regularly visiting with them.

Although a number of physical problems arose during Mr. M's stay at home, we were able to resolve them without much difficulty.

He slowly became physically weaker, but his spirits never flagged. Mrs. M. called regularly about one or more difficulties, but I think in large part, these calls were for her support, not his. They openly discussed his death, funeral arrangements, burial procedures and what life might be like after he was gone. He wanted to make certain changes in his will, made contact with long lost persons, and said his goodbyes. The children openly participated in family planning. Mr. M died quietly at home, about three months after his hospital discharge, in his own bed, sleeping in the room he enjoyed best, overlooking his garden.

Home, children, wife, no hospital corridors, no I.V.s, no nursing home, no hushed feet, no heavy narcotics—such is eminently possible where appropriate conditions exist. Open communication between family and patient and health care staff, directed towards supporting family as well as patient, principally to allow the patient and next-of-kin to mutually support each other, is essential. Open communication allowing a person to express what is on his mind, is the key to participation of self and others, and control within the potential of the limited resources in life. Protection of the ill person almost invariably serves to deny self-participation.

Why should a family wish to protect a loved one from the truth of a fatal illness? One reason is the fear that if the ill person knew of his illness, he would not be able to bear the pain of such truth. He would fall apart, be depressed, or might even attempt suicide. Better to pretend that all is well, especially in the begining of a fatal illness, when symptoms and complaints may be few and partial recovery is possible. Protection of the other may well signify a need to protect oneself. It may be hard for a family member to face the truth in another, for it indicates a truth to oneself, namely that a dissolution and a dying is beginning. To face the losing of a loved one is as frightening and distressing as the illness itself must be for the sick one. It is not only the thought of the loss, but the very problem of how one faces the day-by-day living with the ill and the dying. How can one stand up to the other under such a threat? It is better, obviously, to deny the whole thing. If one pretends that the illness is not fatal, then in fact, perhaps it is not. If a spouse encourages her husband that the situation is improving, maybe all really will turn out well.

Maybe the doctors were wrong, maybe all the rules and regulations about such things do not apply in this case.

As a fatally ill person becomes sicker and more time is spent in the hospital, and less self-control is possible, the same protection oftentimes continues, with the same arguments. Now, an element of embarrassment begins to enter, for the pretense is visibly weaker in the face of reality and harder to maintain. Embarrassment and pretense drive people away from where they are needed. How often can one say, "you look better today" to a person who is obviously failing? How often can one offer expectations that "you'll be on your feet in no time" to a man who has been barely able to leave his bed for some weeks now?

In some circumstances, denying the state of fatalness, or the proximity of death, may allow a spouse to look after the husband or wife at home with minimal conflict. Repression of the awareness of dying may allow a wife to continue to do things for her husband, and to continue allowing him to participate in decisions and plans for the future, as if there were a long future together, without becoming overwhelmingly depressed by the dying process. Even those individuals who are completely aware of the gravity of the illness may prefer to think little of reality while behaving as if recovery were still possible. If such denial or repression allows for care to be given, perhaps it is for the best. But then, the shock of death may be enormous.

The seriously ill and the dying frequently desire to share their thoughts and feelings about illness, about self, about the future, and an understanding physician, minister or nurse may be selected for this sharing. If this sharing can occur, the patient may muster up enough strength and courage to support the pretense of a family unable to participate in this sharing. The competent professional, in this regard, may help support the patient in a manner that the patient may then support his family, Feeling such support, a patient may well play at getting better for the sake of family. To my knowledge however, in the majority of cases, this pretense tends to work both to the impoverishment of the relationship, and to the meaning of intimacy, and subtracts many options otherwise available.

In seminars conducted around issues of the dying and their needs,

I have had young physicians, nurses and nonprofessionals ask about the practical matter of the patient who appears to be dying in a climate of an optimism that he is getting better. What can one do when the staff knows that the patient is dying, as does the family, but the patient seems to want to insist that he is better? The concern is for the gulf that is so created between staff, family and patient.

Many such instances do occur and when they do, supporting the patient's defenses is clearly imperative. In such situations, there is often a staff and family problem as well as a patient problem. The staff may be creating a dissonance by failing to accurately assess the patient's needs. If restlessness, sleeplessness, anxiety, hyperactivity or deep depression is apparent, the defense may be a poor one, and denial is not very successful. If a barrier has been erected to disallow the sick person from openly displaying his knowledge and feelings, a disharmonious state can emerge.

On many occasions I have been told that a terminally ill patient knew nothing about the seriousness of his or her illness and, within a short period of consultation, found myself listening to the patient's awareness of the gravity of the situation, the concerns for children or others after death, and the like. In many instances, so quick an entrance into such delicate but pressing areas of concern does not occur, and patients may desire several visits before feeling confident and trusting enough to openly discuss their deepest concerns and perceptions. This is a matter of trust and willingness on the part of the staff to listen and to "take it."

Also required is a willingness to take it on a family's part. Several years ago a married woman in her late thirties, the mother of two young children, was referred to our unit with a diagnosis of advanced ovarian cancer. She had undergone an exploratory laparotomy a year prior and subsequently had received a course of irradiation treatment to the abdomen. She was fairly well for some time, but symptoms of discomfort and abdominal swelling occurred, and she was referred for chemotherapy by the radiotherapy department, not having seen her surgeon during the previous year. Thus, as she became sicker, she had to establish new working relations with a new group of physicians and nurses.

In her case however, this worked out reasonably well. For a while, she responded well to her chemical treatments but after six months or so, her problems deepened. She began to fail in strength, energy and vitality. Swelling of her legs made ambulation difficult, and swelling of her abdomen caused discomfort and awkwardness of motion. Her appetite lessened, her face became drawn and her ability to do for herself became progressively less. Dependency on others at home became increasingly necessary. She declined several suggestions for hospitalization, relating that her children needed her at home. The decline of her physical ability to do things for the children and for herself reached a point where help at home was required. Her mother-in-law moved in with the family and took over the responsibility of getting the children off to school, preparing meals and generally running the household. She painfully watched her control and effectiveness as a wife and mother diminish. She complained to me that she saw her children only for the quick hello and goodbye in the coming and going to school. Her uselessness weighed heavily upon her, and the despair at her loss of ability to perform was genuine, deep and pathetic to observe.

What seemed the most painful of her many complaints was an inability to discuss her feelings of inadequacy with her husband. For a long time, he continued to share their bed until deciding, with her reluctant approval, (as she became weaker and more uncomfortable) that his tossing and turning might be too much for her. She made several attempts to talk to him about herself, her illness and her failing. With each atempt he would quickly reassure her that she would be getting better soon, and would be able to make up to the children for the time lost. After several such episodes, she stopped attempting to talk to him, limiting conversation to outside events, the weather, mutual friends, the day at the office. She found little sustaining interest in these things, and realized that she had little to say to the children. After a while she barely could talk to her mother-in-law.

Her medical situation progressively deteriorated, and anxiety and physical symptoms mounted. She could hardly sleep or eat, abdominal pains were worsening, requiring more medication, and attacks of shortness of breath even when lying still, were becoming frequent. On occasions when her husband would bring her to the clinic, our conversations assured me that he was well aware of the seriousness of her condition, but felt she had to be encouraged under all circumstances. He felt that as bad as things were, they would be so much worse if hope of getting better was withdrawn.

Some weeks before her death, she was in a most bitter way. I called her husband into the examining room and mildly encouraged her to vent her feelings. He was most uncomfortable, shifting around in his chair. It was pointless, she said, because he wouldn't listen to her, and she could not make him understand. I tried to pinpoint the vagueness by asking her what it was that he couldn't or wouldn't understand, but she could only mutter further about illness and complaints.

After several minutes of this, I gently asked if she was concerned about dying. Her response was a virtual scream of "yes, yes, yes." She had so much to say, so much she wanted to plan with the children, and he wouldn't let her. I helped him to explain that he was really trying to help her as best as he knew how, that he loved her and wanted to protect her, and that he couldn't really see how he would face life without her. I left them mutually crying and comforting each other.

In a fairytale, Mrs. E. would then get better and they would all go down to the seashore and live happily ever after. However, such is not the case with dying; it is seldom easy and never without pain and loss. These two people could draw closer in her last days, use time creatively and meainingfully, but there was still hurt in the loss. The children were now brought in to their mother's life in a warmer and closer way. Goodbyes could be said slowly, but supportively, and hopes and dreams could be imparted to them.

She did not die at home. Her physical problem became so enormous that hospitalization was needed at the end. Her last few days of life were spent with a feeling of belonging to her family, of exercising some influence, limited though it was, over her children's present and future, and in participating in the planning for her funeral and her place of final rest.

For a family member to be able to *take it* means addressing himself to depression, to anger, to jealousy and to pain. Embarrassed by sadness and depression, a family member may wish to bring cheer.

If that does not work, as it seldom does, avoiding the issue by avoiding the patient may be painfully necessary. Since a family member may be depressed personally, avoiding the sick person or the issues around the illness may seem the only thing to do, but often a lack of real communication is so evident. There is a feeling that there is nothing to say to each other. Ideally, a family member should be able to respect the depression, the anger, the jealousy of a sick one, when these emotional states exist, rather than attempt to oppose them. But few can do this without guidance and help either from the medical team, from the minister or from some other trusted source.

As time passes, family members may lag behind the dying loved one in being willing to accept the dying. The patient may have worked through much of his uncertainty and anger, depression and confusion and is now able to face death peacefully, but his family may refuse to acknowledge such acceptance for themselves. As often as one sees families grateful to see the end come to an exhausting illness, there are as often family members who insist on encouraging the patient to improve, refusing to allow the end to come peacefully. Such families will insist that medical care be extended, that something new be tried, that another consultant be called in. Saying goodbye is impossible for them. Patients find themselves in a last minute dilemma, ready to let go and yet conflicting with a loved one. Such lagging often indicates unresolved tensions and frequently requires expert help to work through such tension.

A family that openly shares in the meaning and experiences of dying, can encourage and support the patient's control over his few and limited opportunities to the maximum possible within the physical limitations that exist. Simple things such as letter writing, sitting in a sunny room at home, helping select things to eat, simple chores, can be encouraged if open communication and mutual support exists. Clearly, a profound option is the place of living and dying in the last weeks and days of life, and close communication may well allow a dying person to be comfortably looked after at home (rather than in an institution), provided physical care is reasonable. The feeling of being a burden, so common in many dying patients, can be resolved if one is willing to face the feelings. Decisions are so often made, both in the home or institution, which appear as solutions to problems, but which are really impositions on the sick, emanating from an inability to listen to the words and feelings of the sick or of a family member.

Being able to listen, and attempting to understand, may permit the patient to find a path towards meaningful living. But as already stated, for a family to tolerate and try to resolve the anger and depression may be difficult if not impossible, without professional guidance and help. It may even be difficult when such help is available. Often there are no real answers to the human problem of dying. In our problem-oriented culture, we like to look at various human phenomena as problems to be solved by the application of technology and professional skills. Serious life issues are less problems than events, not open to quick solution by an applied skill. Rather, modest changes are possible in certain life events by a gradual improvement in understanding, and in coping with the crisis.

Even when death is near, help in changing family dynamic may be possible. Consolation, empathy and compassion can be encouraged. A family may work towards that unity and support that allows the sick one to move through his anger and depression to reach that state of accepting fate's blows and to participate as best he can in his limited life. As stated several times, families unfortunately are so fixed in their ways and styles, that resolution of these types of problems are not possible without help for both the patient and for themselves.

Families frequently fail to recognize that help is needed. This is especially true in the psychologic sphere. There still exists a rather strong feeling, especially among the less "intellectualized," that problems are one's own and should be solved by one's own capabilities. Psychologic counseling is for the "crazy." If conflicts get out of hand or if chaos emerges, then some kinds of help may become acceptable. But in dealing with fatal illness and the dying, families seldom perceive themselves in trouble, and seldom actively seek help. Even when help is volunteered they may well feel suspicious and untrusting, and will reject an offered hand at first.[5]

If the helping hand to deal with these psychologic and social issues were an integral part of the health care in chronic and fatal illness, and were so organized that each family would be included in some helping program, probably initiated at a hospital or clinic, then gradually resistance would diminish, and the concept that fatal illness is a stress on families and requires help, would become acceptable. For today however, the situation remains that families do not expect much in the way of exploration of their feelings and behavior, and often resist the notion that they should use available facilities, scant as these may be.

Once again let me emphasize that an open communication between family members, often aided by professional guidance, is generally the best guarantee of allowing a patient to stay in control of his limited resources and feel esteemed, worthy and loved. Unresolving anger and misunderstood depression assuredly block communication. Open communication may be impossible in all circusmtances, and yet is desired as the one effective way of eventually dispelling these affects.

Some degree of denial and repression of reality may be needed in certain families to allow for functioning in the crisis of dying. There are people whose life styles have been to hide away in the face of dangers, either by running away from them or by denying that they exist. Such a person may never be able to confront his mortality by openly discussing it, and could never deal with his family unless by denial. How does one know when the support of such denial is to be preferred? The answer is not simple, because simply not talking about something important is not denial. There must be opportunity to talk about the issue.

Guidance in this area must be from the sick one himself. If he is allowed to set the pace of what is to be shared, and is encouraged rather than repudiated in doing so, it will soon be apparent if the person is denying or simply protecting. If the issue is truth in communicating, then truth must be seen as a flexible word requiring that tact, patience and grace be appended to it. Truth can be shared in small increments, and the sick individual can be allowed to digest, absorb and grow into truth. This principle holds true for family members as well as patients. Even at the ending of one's life, constancy in truth and awareness may not exist, and it is not infrequent that families become confused by a patient who will one day talk about where he would like to be buried, and the next wintry day be talking about planting new bushes next spring. While on one hand the dying may seem to be at ease fully accepting giving over life, there may be an insistence that there be anticipation of a future. This ambivalence is common in the dying, and should not be surprising.

It is hard to stare resolutely into one's death, and future thinking is so much a part of our value structure and training. If we allow a person this ambivalence, we understand and accept the posssibility that even in a full acquiescence to dying, some looking for a future is human. Ambivalence is not denial, and one should not feel that a person is still struggling or has not found peace, if this type of ambivalence is seen. It can be supported lovingly and genuinely. Frequently, if a dying person has aired his awareness of his condition, and has found loving support and trust in the environment, there may be little further need to talk of dying, and talk of the living may be in order. This obviously is not pretense. It is simply the acceptance that things are in the open and need not be dwelled upon continuously. A family needs to understand where the patient "is at" and where the other family members are at if the communion and support is to exist.

For many people, biological death of a near family member may be sad, but not really a loss. There are families in which relationships were not gratified through love and growth, but in which pain, punishment and disorganization marked the lives of those in the group. Rather than finding love and support in one's parents, a child may feel that betrayal, severity, hate and resentment long replaced caring as a description of family life.

Such individuals may do their duty to mother or father or spouse during a fatal illness, but the eventual death may signify little but a sense of relief for such people, crying and mourning may have little meaning; others in the family may rise in anger and resentment at the absence of "appropriate" behavior, accusing the person of heartlessness, emptiness, less-than-humanness. Such accusation may result in the further rupture of relationships already tenuous, although it may well be that such accusation stems more from guilt reactions and unresolved conflicts within the accusers than from true loving of the deceased. Anger can result from failure to keep up appearances.

Through this chapter the accent has been on the family helping a loved one to die peacefully. This objective, considered only in its own terms, is worthy beyond question. But there certainly is more to such an objective, for it is in the style and nature of a person's death that he is remembered. It takes courage to face one's death and come through the victor. It requires style to see, in dying, the last fulfillment of meaning in life. Such courage and style, when seen, serves us well as a lesson for our own deaths.

It has been said that though death destroys us, the knowledge and manner of one's death can save us. Those who continue to live can take pride in the manner of a loved one's dying. Peace at the end can mean a peace in the living. So much adjustment is needed in families after a death, that the presence or absence of peace in death can severly affect the mourning process. Loss is hard to live with, and when unresolved tensions and struggles mark the last days of a life, survivors have a deep wound that will continue long afterwards. A peaceful dying will not resolve subsequent loneliness and hurt, but will help to ease the psychological burden of surviving.

The older a person is at the time of dying, the easier the consequences, as a general rule. Social tasks have been accomplished, such as child rearing, homemaking, careers and community leadership. Children have taken on new love relationships in their own families. The death of the very elderly seems to imply the completion of life. But generalities suffer many exceptions and where dependent relations still hold, no time is ripe time. Somebody will suffer. The remaining spouse often has nothing to live for, and children and grandchildren cannot seem to fill the void. Suicide being unacceptable, one often sees old people sitting and waiting to die, waiting to be reunited in death with a lost love, or to lie in eternal peace, side by side.

There probably is no way to answer such loneliness and expectancy, except to be aware of it. What must be protected against is unnecessary brutality and further betrayal in life. To find ways of helping such lonely elders to an ease in living, and a sense of dignity, is a task our society has overlooked to date. Despair in the last winters of life means a mockery of civilization. Death at any age younger than the most elderly is inappropriate by our standards, yet, what is elderly and what is not, is totally arbitrary. If death is to come, we must work to make it meaningful and appropriate within its own context, for only then can we continue to live fully as meaningful humans.

[1]Silverman, Phyllis R.: Widowhood and preventive intervention. *The Family Coordinator,* January, 1972.

[2]Parkes, C. Murray: Effects of bereavement in physical and mental health— A study of the medical records of widows. *British Medical Journal, 2:*274, 1964.

[3]Parkes, C. Murray: The first year of bereavement—A longitudinal study of the reaction of London widows to the death of their husbands. *Psychiatry, 33:* 444-467, 1970.

[4]Gorer, Geoffrey: *Death, Grief and Mourning.* Garden City, N.Y., Doubleday, 1965. A study of contemporary society.

[5]My present work with dying patients and their families indicates that about 40 percent of families contacted reject an offer for help. This is especially true for husbands of ill wives. Similar experiences following a death have been noted by R. Volleman, A. Ganzert, L. Picher, and A. Williams in The reactions of family systems to sudden and unexpected death. *Omega: International Journal for the Psychological Study of Dying, Death, Bereavement, Suicide and Other Lethal Behaviors, 2:*101-105, 1971.

CHAPTER VII

SOME PROPOSALS FOR EDUCATION

W HEN ONE SPEAKS of education, the question is usually posed as one of specificity, namely, of what and for which group? We seldom think of education as a broad firmament in which basic human problems can be explored as a phenomenon common to all men. Although we still have a general education format in primary and secondary schools, the colleges and universities have become places for specialization, and professional graduate schools accentuate the funneling of education into precise but narrow areas, each intensely important, but each separate from the other, committed and devoted to producing a graduate well skilled in his special area, but with little understanding of the world of another's function and thought.

Human crisis, needless to say, is something all men endure, and the faces of death and dying, of grieving and suffering, disturb us all. "For no man shall be born who shall not see death." Death unites us all in common heritage and truth, but we find ourselves divided into innumerable camps when attempting to deal with it. Those with power may control the deaths of the powerless in a manner that robs life of all meaning. Religions may persuade us that heaven is limited only to adherents of a specific credo. Some scientists may be convinced that death is simply the inadequacy of a scientific understanding of human biology.

It is probably safe to assume that death was easier to understand and tolerate in a society that was firmly rooted in values, traditions, rituals and religion. Where most, if not all people in a particular society looked at living and life's problems through traditional and culturally common eyes, death belonged to all men together and suffering could be commonly supported within the group. It was not that men did not fear and did not suffer from loss, but it was that help and support were present in the larger community of men simply by belonging and by believing in the belonging. There was something more to a man than the singular "I."

In some primitive societies, the death of a hunter might clearly implicate that the death of a dependent spouse was now anticipated, especially if no alternate life support, by children for example, was forthcoming. But even this was put into the context of tribal or group behavior, and all understood and functioned, even though suffering, in that understanding.

It is obvious, however, that these older and more coherent cultures and societies were not enough for men, for time has seen so many of them eroded and discarded by new designs for living through the growth of materialism, technology, science, and individualism. In the United States we have grown up with the political philosophy that each man is individual, self-dependent, self-growing, free to compete for the good things and for social position, and free to suffer the consequences of failure. Dying in many ways has become an individual problem with each person in each family, now loosened from older moralities, rituals and traditions, struggling to find a personal meaning and to more or less hide his suffering from a society basically inhospitable to pain.

Our professional educational system tends to accentuate and exaggerate this singularity and loneliness. Colleges and universities develop educational programs or curricula rather early in a student's life, and although there is certainly some mixing, physics majors may quickly move off into their specialized concerns in preparation for graduate school training, leaving the chemists to their paths, the pre-meds to theirs. Schools of theology, of medicine, of engineering, of architecture, of nursing, of social work, of sociology, gather in their students and tend to keep them there, away from others, arguing that the pressure of professional education is too intense and time is too limited, even for the voluminous material distinct to each specialty.

In the health area this is especially true. For all the low level humor of the sexual mixing of medical and nursing students, the two disciplines are typically kept far from each other in the formative years of professional development. While the two are commonly placed in a common working habitat, they seldom know how to communicate meaningfully with each other. They tend to go their separate ways, but not free of rancor, confusion and frustration.

In hospitals, doctors tend to communicate with nurses via order books, with little concern for the driving professional and personal needs of the latter. Nurses may become frustrated and angry with medical decisions, with particular physicians, with a particular medical system, but find that they have no way of redressing such discomforts, nor do many of them feel at all daring to do so. In the hospital non-mix, laboratory technicians, nursing aides, social workers, ministers and many others wander about the institution with supposed singular professional performances, acting in their particular professional arena, zealously guarding their professional stances and rights, angry at their powerlessness relative to professional administrators and possessive physicians.

Nowhere is this separation of purpose and performance more visible and painful than in the area of the dying person. Not acutely, for in cases of accidents or sudden disaster to the previously healthy, everyone seems to know their roles and to be cooperative and amenable. However in fatal illness, a professional separation and apartness both produces and enhances anguish and pain for all, especially for the patient and his family. A physician concerned with promoting a new treatment or another test may be unaware of the smoldering resentment of a nurse attempting to protect a patient against maneuvers. A minister may find himself robbed of an effective role by being denied information as to the status of a patient, or by being denied entry into a dying patient's room where "emergency" procedures are being performed by a physician. A social worker may throw up her hands in dismay at being initially requested to see a patient who is about to be discharged, and with whom there is little or no time for truly helping.

The dying and their families need a coordinated, safe environment, but our educational system virtually guarantees that such a setting will come about more by accident than by design. For people to work effectively together they must be acquainted with each other's capabilities and purposes, with each other's concepts of the roles they see themselves performing, and with each other's needs to participate in decision making and responsibility sharing. In any working arrangement, if power for decision making and role assignment is in the hands of only one person, as benevolent as he may be, resentment and confusion will emerge if others see themselves as powerless to initiate change as they might wish it. This certainly includes the patient since dying is more than simply succumbing to a biologic disease, but is the ending of a singular man's personal life. Decisions to be made about the dying process must clearly include the person's right to participate in deciding.

We need an educational design in health areas, though perhaps in all human crisis areas, where students in different educational facilities can come together for several hours of each academic week to share and discuss major issues. The meaning of dying must be seen through the eyes of all who will professionally have something to do with a dying person, and must be a shared educational experience. The young medical student must come to understand what a nursing student, theology student, social service student, perceives as his or her role, contributions, fears, problems. Architects design the buildings that will house the sick, the dying, the families who come visiting. These institutions tend to be constructed as if personal human needs could be easily obliterated or discounted. There exists a need for light, for gardens, for a quiet spot to meditate, a corner where a family might share a meal without the need for going to the coin-operated canteen or cafeteria, a place where a spouse might sleep over. Young architectural students should be exposed to other students for sharing, discussing, getting to know the other.

Opportunities to continue a common dialogue around issues of human caring should continue as students mature and proceed into their senior years. Such study opportunities should expose methods of decision making, and reviewing power arrangements between specialties, allowing for a full understanding of what a professional role is, and how complicated social and professional arrangements operate in a hospital setting. Not only must human psychology and sociology be stressed, but meaning in human life must be explored and such phenomena as truth, courage, justice, love, compassion and dignity enjoined. The development of skills in perceiving human hurt and frailty and the empathetic management and counselling of patients and families must be stressed.

These same learning methods should be applied as skills to help and support fellow professionals and others, aiming principally for easy and open communication with each other, support for each other, easing of the fears in each other, and the enhancement of the esteem of each other. To be requested and permitted to participate in human tragedy requires the responsibility of gathering appropriate information about another's life, and open and free professional communication as a major *right*. This right implies that the decision making process be a shared commitment and not limited to biologic decisions exclusively. Professionals have their own fears and frights, and can seldom do a good job unless these can be gently exposed in a supporting, interhuman fashion.

I am most concerned that we return a man's life and dying to him, to the maximum that he can participate in the area of decision. All personnel have an important role to play in supporting this position. A simple example would be the decision of when and how to control pain. If a patient complains of severe physical pain and it is clear that good physical reason exists to explain this pain, drugs of various kinds are frequently employed to ease or eradicate the disturbance. Many drugs, especially opiates such as morphine, may cause alterations in consciousness that once initiated, may remove awareness and inhibit active thinking.

This may be a sensible price to pay from the physician's viewpoint, but we cannot be sure that the nurses always agree, nor can we be sure that the patient would always agree, if allowed to participate in a meaningful decision-making process. To be meaningful, the patient should be informed of the probable somnolence or floating sensation produced by the medication, and allowed to decide if this is what he really wishes. It is quite conceivable that some degree of pain might be tolerated if an active and alert mental status were deemed important. A physician should not have the right to impose a drug decision without consulting with the patient. All too frequently, especially in institutions, pain relieving medications and drugs such as tranquilizers, are administered to patients eager for some relief without discussion of the possible mental consequences.

Pain is a particularly difficult problem for the patient, for his family and for a staff to tolerate, and obliteration of pain and patient together, may be considered acceptable at any price by the physician or nurse. This clearly robs the patient of a right to his pain if mental activity is deeply desired. Warm and empathetic physicians are naturally, aware of this, but professional educational systems make little attempt to demand the inherent right of patients to maximum control of their lives and environments. It is probably true that most people are so frightened by pain, are so dependent upon the physician, that alteration in consciousness may be easily accepted and unargued. Many may even wish for the obliteration that drugs provide, not just from pain but from any contact with reality. Such a response is a running into anxiety and emptiness, and if any dignity is to emerge, the individual needs enormous personal contact and help.

In many other areas, decisions are frequently forced on patients in attempts to improve them biologically with little consideration for the psychological or family consequences. Again, this is not done out of malice, nor aimed at anything but the best in medical caregiving. The difficulty arises from the lack of in-depth education as to the way a person perceives of his needs, and an understanding of the magnitude of the insult to his self-esteem, so common in all illnesses but especially in fatal illness. Medical education so often proceeds as if illness is the same as disease, and that treating disease is not just the key objective but the only objective. This perspective is a technical one, and technology of this type can only be successful by assuming that men are in fact concerned only with the molecular and the exact. An illness is more than a disease, and a dying is more than an unconquered defect in biology.

The poets, writers, playwrights and artists have always understood this and have struggled to put into words and onto canvasses that which was both deeply personal and universally human in living and dying. Theology and the ministries have understood the human anguish in living and dying, and have tried to create universal appeals to the mystical and metaphysical side of man's nature as a buttress against cruel and cataclysmic life. Yet, the arts and religion are seldom included in the education of the health professional. If the sensitive physician or nurse searches the heart of literature, poetry, philosophy or painting for help in struggling with issues of mortality or in fact, any human crisis, he or she does so on his own time. Such effort is little appreciated by school administrators or hospital directors.

The inclusion of poetry, literature, religion and philosophy into the curriculum of medicine and nursing should become mandatory, specifically as issues of fatal illness, crippling and disfiguring illness, dying, mourning and suffering are discussed. This is more than psychology or psychiatry, for the latter take their origins in singular humans reacting to problems, while art carries with it an attitude toward the pain and joy of all humans. The language of psychology is positivistic, giving rise to interpretation, measurement, direction towards conceived hypothetical principles or theories. The language of art is personal yet universal, rooted in experience, and demands that what a person experiences is as correct and reasonable in itself as is any preestablished notion of what is good and what is bad through theoretic generalities.

Modern psychologists are pleading for a new authenticity in measuring human behavior, called autopsychology by some, peak-experience existentialism by others.[1] The names are not important, but the belief is that what goes on in a human as personal experience is as real and authentic and profound and good, even if that experience is into the mystical, the cosmic, the transcendental. This ability of a person to be outside the rational, the ordinary, the constrained, and into a deeper feeling for life, is what the capable artist has frequently known, and has tried to crystallize with his particular art language. These art languages can be extremely awakening, and are most needed to stir into conscious awareness the depth of human joy and suffering, and some of the ultimate meanings of life and death.

The young professional health care student needs exposure to the others in his broad health professional undertaking. He needs exposure to other languages than the biologic for dealing with illness and dying. The young health professional needs another strategy for the dying than the simple alternatives of treating for recovery until the end, or abandoning when little more "medically" can be done.

It would appear that the expansion of scientific and biologic information is so wide and intense, that there is little time to train the physician to be at home in human suffering apart from the technologic dimensions. This problem would become further accentuated by shortening of the medical curriculum from four years to three, now proposed as the mechanism for producing more physicians for a nation said to be laboring under a doctor shortage. Added to this time-demand problem will be the medical demands of a continually increasing number of older citizens, as many more reach their later years than formerly possible, with their generally greater need for medical care. The concern with making good medical care available to the poor, the disadvantaged, the inner city ghettoes, will also require new distribution of physicians and nurses. These major efforts in acute medical problems may serve to diminish the concern to define man in his human qualities when fatal illness is present, even if we acknowledge that these issues are most pressing and should not be minimized.

Perhaps we must educate a new type of professional, one whose primary role is human advocacy in disease. A professional of this nature will be trained to understand physical illness, and trained as well to understand how decisions are made in caregiving. This professional will not need in-depth training in pharmacology, biochemistry, anatomy, but will be required to be well trained in psychology, sociology, and reasonably alive to religion, philosophy and the arts. He should be schooled in group dynamics and social process. He should be fully aware of the tasks and responsibilities of the other professionals with whom he will work and understand the fulfillment needs of the professionals he will be in contact with. He will be required to have insight into the cultural pressures of patients he will be looking after and will have labored to master family dynamics and counselling. He will be required to recognize when a presenting medical problem is in reality a biologic issue, requiring good medical technicologic intervention, and when a problem is more humanistic, requiring other resources to be employed. Many times the questions at stake will not be clear, and will require considerable thought and discussion before adequate decisions can be reached.

In the area of fatal illness, just such a professional is sorely needed. In the early stages of a fatal disease such as lung cancer, there are definite medical procedures needed to diagnose the illness, and to stage the extent of the illness. Has it metastasized? To what area?

What is the general prognosis in terms of time left to live (roughly)? In certain situations, medical treatments are clearly indicated, for surgery or radiation treatments may be curative and have good reason to be used.

In the later stages of lung cancer and toward the terminal stages of illness, a gray zone exists. Certain drug treatments may help but frequently do not. Some ability to select the right patient for the right drugs exists today, but unfortunately, this capacity is sharply limited. Drugs may cause many side effects. Many new, experimental drugs and procedures are presently available and many more will be forthcoming as medical researchers explore new methods of treatment. Physicians interested in testing these new agents may push them on to patients and their families, with really the best disease-oriented interests and kindly concern for patients, but with starkly limited humanistic alternatives. Patients themselves, with their dependency relationships with their physicians, have little opportunity to explore alternatives and frequently find themselves with no options but to go along with the treatment decision, for fear that refusing will result in either abandonment or in foreclosing of fantasized possibilities.

It is in this latter gray zone that the "other-than-biologic" ways of helping patients must be explored, and the requirement is for this new professional to both understand and enforce these alternatives. These alternatives do not exclude the use of experimental procedures. Instead they support the ability of the patient to fully understand what is happening and to allow the opportunity of selecting for himself what he would wish. If the chances of the disease improving with this new procedure are only one in five or less, and the time of improvement probably no more than a few weeks or a month, and the price of being treated is hospitalization, many unpleasant side effects, or possible shortening of remaining life, that ill individual must be helped to say no to the new drug without fearing retaliation through abandonment. Is there a trip he would rather have, a task to be done, a summing up he would prefer?

A neutral professional, uncommited to the experimental treatment, but fully committed to the patient, may be able to assist in making the decision appropriate for him and his personal needs, without the threat of abandonment nor the implication that things are hopeless.

Who should this new professional be? In some ways we are describing a psychiatrist, but that description pales as we recognize that most psychiatrists are wedded to psychiatric disorders and not to physical problems. Nevertheless the tasks outlined for such a person most comfortably fit a "mind-oriented" individual who assumedly, could be trained in a department of psychiatry or psychology, if the right attention were given to developing the role. On the other hand, we could be describing the physician, if many of the technical roles of medicine could be assigned to others, either a more technically oriented physician or to physician assistants.

There is ample opportunity for such a development, for new instrumentation in medicine may well offer the possibility of viewing education as a search for human being and inter-being, rather than as merely a mechanistic dissection of the person into separate organs and cell systems. Computerization may well be visualized as the new technicologic magic, making fact retrieval and mechanical pursuits easier and allowing a new freedom to deal with behavioral issues. The computer can help the physician in the solution of a problem, releasing available time for engaging in the meaning of person and illness. Machinery however, has its own intrinsic fascination, and the computer may serve only to excite a new special mechanical vision of human trouble, creating rewarding problem solving and improved medical care in small as well as large communities, but further tunneling the professional's vision as to what constitutes human tragedy.

Unless our educational systems become geared to the problems of the dying as a specific area of need, the physician will not likely be the figure under discussion. But should he be it would greatly ease the transitions which would have to take place in power arrangements now existing. Doctors generally do not like to think of themselves as merely technicians and needless to say, the better physicians neither think nor act that way. To be privy to human pain and hurt demands understanding, patience, tact and most of all, acceptance of the obligations that intimacy demands. Availability, continuity, thoughtful counselling, support of esteem—all of these and more, as well as skills in biology and technology, are demanded.

Control of decision making rests in the physician's hands today, and he is most zealous in guarding this right. Not only does such control afford the narcissistic reward of being "the great one," but supposedly this power comes about because the physician is the most knowing person caring for a patient. It is to him that the patient and family turn in times of trouble. He is seen by the public as the possessor of knowledge and the intervener for correction of problems. He has fostered the view that only he can bear this responsibility. In a way he is correct, but only in certain ways. When I was in Sweden recently, the issue of misuse of physicians was raised, as in the field of obstetrics. Midwifery is extensively used in Sweden and a gynecologist informed me that her own children had been delivered by midwives. Physicians are seldom used, quite contrary to American practice. Trained midwives are quite capable of deciding when the expert help of a physician is required and when not. Counselling and support are offered by the midwife.

In a nonprivate institutional setting, the idea of a new guiding professional should not be difficult to envision. The selection of patients for whom he will bear primary responsibility will certainly offer little difficulties if we limit our concepts now to fatal disease. Many fatal illnesses may last months to years and early participation would be vastly preferred than later. In as much as one of the key charges of this professional is coordinated planning with nurses, social workers, ministers and other staff as well as with technical medicine, the earlier such planning begins the better for staff and patient. Ongoing care and counselling may be assigned to one specific staff member as a social worker, working closely with physicians and surgeons as well as with families.

Again, it is not that social workers do not work with physicians and families now, but rather that the power and trust to make decisions and to direct those decisions into humanistic rather than technical areas does not now exist, and should become the objective of the program for the dying. As the terminal period draws to a close and as new and intense issues for patient and family arise, as they do for nurses, ministers and physicians, these will best be managed if seen as part of an already ongoing process, aimed at supporting human capacity and dignity in hospitals and homes and in the enhancement of a peaceful dying.

Much greater attention will have to be given to home programs than now exists. The trend in medical care today is to focus greater and greater resources in the institution, and less and less in the home. If a hospital is to be the central agent for caregiving in the community, it must logically become wall-less. Creation of teams of helpers to support home care need not be thought of as nonhospital roles, but as a natural extension of already existing hospital facilities. Several institutions in the Boston area do have coordinated home care programs, but they represent a liaison with Visiting Nurse Associations rather than outreaching hospital programs in which all professional members participate. It is still difficult to get hospital-based physicians to make house calls. Even the most supportive and loving family would have difficulty caring for a terminally ill loved one at home without the safe feeling of a medical unit capable of responding to need. Medical economics and third party insurance programs will require revision so that legitimate home care can be reimbursed, which is not the case at present. The present insurance arrangements work against home care and force institutional dying for many.

Private institutions, community institutions and the entire system of fee-for-service private practice of medicine is another order of magnitude. Some of the best and most extensive medical care is given in these community hospitals, dominated and controlled by the private practitioner. Patients tend to be considered as "private" and most times wish to be so, right to the end of life. Although I have no data, my feeling is that this privacy does not assure the dying patient and his family a better resource for concluding life.

Not too long ago I was invited to a lovely community hospital, approximately twenty miles west of Boston to plan for a series of conferences on the issues of the dying patient. It was the nursing staff that extended the invitation. Several physicians were present as were two or three ministers and two social workers. After some discussion, one of the physicians turned to me and pointed out that in the community hospitals attention to problems such as dying were handled vastly better than in the big city hospitals, for people really "cared" in the suburbs. Whereupon one of the social workers indignantly announced that in her eighteen months of working at the hospital, not once had she been consulted or utilized for a patient or family around issues of dying and death. Did the physician indeed attend well to the psychologic and social issues?

It will take considerable education to convince the physician that something better can be done for the patient and his family around the probems of dying and grieving, and to convince citizens that they deserve something better.

A colleague once asked if there was anything more to taking care of a dying person than good medical care and consideration of the family. The answer of course is yes. Good medical care is usually seen as doing medical things such as tests, injections and pills. If someone is depressed, tranquilizers; if unable to sleep, pills. However, if someone wants to talk for an hour or so there is no time, or there is the psychiatrist. Physicians are not unkind and they certainly want to do the best they can. They work long, hard hours doing their tasks. Dealing with psychologic tensions in patients and families is hard at best, and exhausts too much time. Confrontations with the dying are often too traumatic and shaking. Ongoing care of family members after a death gets registered as physical care, such as tranquilizers, sleeping pills and the like. Understanding of the grief process with the conflicts, guilt, anger and defenses against pain inherent therein is far from common, and application of medical skills to routinely counsel and assist family members is seldom available.

There has been some suggestion that the facilitating of appropriate mourning processes in grieving families at the time of death may protect against deleterious health disturbances in later life.[2] Generally, little is provided today, hospitals and physicians taking almost no responsibility for family grief resolution after a death. The ministry appears to do a meager job at best. Education into grief and its subsequent outcomes is much in need among health professionals, along with expanded roles in preventive medicine around these issues. Good medical care means awareness and action into these human areas of perceived need. For this to happen, a new educational design for an expanded health concept will have to be developed, and new coordinated programs initiated.

With more and more community health problems focusing on the hospital as the central designer and deliverer of care, family oriented preventive medical programs, as well as truly operational home care programs, need to be designed. Not only should the hospitals become wall-less in the sense of the development of coordinated care at home, but the responsibility of ongoing concern for the family after a death should be assumed. Many families can make it through a loss reaction without much outside help, especially if a rich network of intra-familial and community links exist. Frequently this is not the case and many legal, social, as well as psychological problems arise that need coordinated help.

Some community agencies do exist, but the bereaved do not know how to employ them, nor are there outreaching services designed to search for and find these needy. The hospital can become the base for such ongoing programs by coordinating church social groups, social security agencies, widow programs and the like. If desired, the hospital could serve only as the resource agency. However, I believe it has a powerful opportunity to see itself as a true total health facility by becoming an active participant, through the creation of a community medical unit or a human crisis unit. Physicians, psychiatrists, psychologists, lawyers, ministers, nurses, social workers, volunteer widows and widowers and others can join and participate. Continued contact with families can be maintained and the general principles of preventive medicine in human crisis employed.

These programs require money, but perhaps even more than economy is an understanding of need, not in terms of institutions, but of people. We must examine many hallowed hospital practices in an attempt to understand for whose benefit they exist. Why, for example, are children not permitted to visit in many institutions? Are they restricted so that they may be protected from exposure to human suffering? If so, why? Are they restricted because they get in the way? Whose? Do they interfere with hospital function by making noise? Why not restrict or restrain the noisy children only? It is truly beneficial to prevent a dying woman from seeing her under-twelve-year-old child, or to prevent the child from seeing its mother?

Why do we not let pets into institutions? Do dogs carry in filth that people do not with their shoes, coats and hands? Is a dog so basically diseased that a patient would be made sicker? Then why not throw pets out of homes when people become ill? Will a pet contaminate other patients? Will it start fights, make noise and disrupt the hospital? Will a dog urinate in the corridor? Perhaps, but if so, an area could be set up in the institution for pets visiting, and rules and regulations enacted to restrict untrained animals. For many dying people, a pet is a critical family member.

Why do we not encourage family members to participate in care-giving and to sleep over, if they wish, by providing space for them? There are some pediatric live-in units for parents of critically ill children. Should not an adult have the same opportunity? Is it only money that stops it? Family members may well get in the way, may well watch critically while procedures are done, may well exhaust themselves. But they can be guided and helped to understand the nurses' or doctors' roles. Helping and being there is so important for so many. Telling a husband that there is nothing more he can do when his wife is dying is to completely misunderstand his need simply to be there.

Many more institutional practices need critical examination, especially around the issues of dying and bereavement. The way medicines are controlled, the way pain is relieved, the emphasis on autopsy requests for the sake of pathologic completeness—all need review. The latter point is particularly irksome. For a loving family, the moment of death is an extraordinarily difficult one. At one moment a person is still alive, but the next, dead. That conceptual transition is often exquisitely difficult. The dead are profane in one way and the undertaker's job is to care for the empty shell. But in another way, the dead stay alive. Families frequently mumble statements like, "she suffered enough" or, "he wouldn't want that," indicating a feeling that there is still a human presence.

While there are many sophisticated people for whom an autopsy is acceptable as another important medical procedure, for many others an autopsy is a violation on that still existing person. The young house officer who applies pressure for "medicine's sake," or the "family's safety," is completely failing to comprehend the intense conflict and concern in a next-of-kin that might well lead to considerable psychologic anguish afterwards if a "yes" is forced. Autopsies are important and useful, but not at the price of a subsequent feeling of guilt.

It is eminently true that teaching and training of professionals interested in health care, especially in areas where dying people are frequently met, must be changed if peaceful dying is to become routine. We need also to examine personal concepts about death and dying, and to change an educational pattern for our children, young adults and mature adults themselves in the areas of human suffering. Death education generally, is considered taboo, a mystery, a vanity or a non-necessity. Many of the problems besetting health care, causing confusion and disorder, come from attempting to assign to the physician a role and job that truly belongs elsewhere. Dying is not essentially medicine's problem. Making people better in the cure or containment of disease is today's medical purpose and any other problem, handed by default to medicine, will be forced to alter its shape and appearance to fit in the molded designs of curing and containing. How a man dies is society's problem, unless the society in general wishes to renege on its obligation, and allow dying to be solely the failure of being cured or contained.

A number of issues have been before the public in the past few years relating to questions of death. In the main, these questions have been mechanistic. They range from problems of pulling the cord, being dead for transplantation purposes, and arguments for euthanasia in the sense of a pact for death. The "pulling of the cord" question has come about because of the development of machinery, mostly electronic, that can keep certain mechanical functions of the body going, such as a pacemaker to make the heart contract, a respirator that will drive the lungs to expand, or intravenous fluids to drip into veins of dehydrated or unconscious people. Most such devices were invented as aids to acute medical problems, where recovery would be possible if a sudden physiological alteration could be overcome.

A person experiencing an acute heart attack might develop a sufficiently critical acute injury to a specific part of the heart to result in cessation of the natural electrical impulse that causes the heart ventricular muscle to contract. The temporary use of a cardiac heart stimulator might well help the patient through that crisis, until the self-regulatory system took over again. An extension of this application occurs when small artificial pacemakers can be permanently installed and maintained in those situations where damage to the natural conduction system was permanent but the heart otherwise viable. The availability of machinery led to its application when a person might be slowly dying of heart or other disease and where in effect, consciousnes or awareness might have disappeared for some time while

the machine continued biologic life through activation of the circulatory system.

To pull the cord would mean to end that biologic impulse called
life. To continue using the machine maintains life. One can always
fantasize for the recovery as long as life is there in some form. Who
can make the decision to end the thread of life if the possibility is
dangled that just perhaps some improvement may occur? If the
patient were conscious, would a plea for discontinuing these external
resuscitative mechanisms be granted? If the patient is unconscious,
can a next-of-kin exercise that right? Dare he to end the life of a
loved one himself without enduring guilt, despair, or blame? Yet,
can he tolerate watching life go on this way? How will the physician
help in that decision? Should he do it on his own, or after conferring
with the family and telling them what decision he has reached, and
asking if anyone would really wish it differently? Or should he place
the burden for decision solely on the family?

When to pull the cord and who should pull the cord are debated
today, but scarcely sufficiently. Nevertheless, the argument truly does
not rest there. It must begin in an entirely other dimension, namely,
what right does a person and his family have to a peaceful and meaningful death? The end mechanics are now the argument, but these
problems emanate from the failure of a thought-out debate on meaningful life and meaningful death. The physician or family may well
find themselves accused of playing God by interfering with a machine's
function. But it is unclear whether God intended man to be kept
mechanically alive when otherwise no longer a person. If God helps
man to build machines, He must also give man the right to decide
when to use or push aside these inventions.

Transplantation of human organs remains in a highly experimental
phase, but it is already clear that the donation of a part of one's body
and the inclusion of this part into another's body is not a simple mechanical event, even if all the rejecting mechanisms existing in the
singular recipient's body can be overcome. There are enormous psychological problems, but that is not fruit for this discussion. The tran-
plantation of an organ such as a heart, requires one man's death.
Concern must exist as to when medicine decides that the potential
donor has truly died or must inevitably die, so that the organ can be

obtained. If a heart must be transplanted at the moment of death and not later, a defense against premature or unnecessary death must be mounted. We thus find ourselves in argument against too early a giving up of one life for the experimental sake of another.

The arguments for today's euthanasia are well known. No person should be forced to suffer excessively from physical pain or distress and since the taking of one's own life is so difficult if not nearly impossible for most, a trusting pact is to be made to ensure that continuing or long-enduring suffering need not go on indefinitely. Giving another the right to proceed and administer a lethal solution or medication requires considerable trusting that an abuse of this granted power over one's life will not occur.

Exactly when one will have had enough suffering to proceed with rapid death needs clear definition in any euthanasia compact. If the plan has been inaugurated at a time when the involved individual is in good health and not ill with a fatal diagnosis, then the individual(s) made responsible for the final administration of the lethal dose or withholding of a technicologic procedure after the fatal illness has been diagnosed and the anticipated suffering has begun, must be constantly alert to any implicit or explicit signal that the ill individual now confronting the immediacy of the prearranged pact, wishes to be released from induced fatality. And I believe this may happen frequently. There is a clinging to living that is frequently found that belies any intellectual readiness conceived at any time prior to the confrontation with death.

I vividly remember a middle-aged woman some years ago, who developed a gastrointestinal cancer that was inoperable and quickly led to a series of painful and distressing abdominal complaints that could only be moderately palliated with medication and various tubes in various orifices. Her strength weakened rapidly in the hospital and after calling her family together, she said appropriate goodbyes and then asked to die. There had been no euthanasia discussion prior nor any arrangements made, although for several days prior to this announcement she had told several of the medical staff that if she wasn't to get better, there really would be no point to prolonging her life with tubes, intravenous fluids and pain medication. Her request to "have it over" was for an immediate solution.

We gently told her that we would not prolong her life by any exceptional action, but that we could not just give her a large dose of a potentially lethal drug. Our talk was lengthy, ranging from ethics to the law, but essentially we promised not to let her experience excessive pain. Her narcotic dose was increased, a tranquilizer added and sleeping medication increased so that she spent the next several days drowsing most of the time. However, not only did she not die, but gave many indications that she could not die yet. She would wake up and start calling for her family, she would request fluids frequently for an unmitigated thirst. Even when apparently sleeping, her hands were tightly clenched as though holding on, clutching to life.

After several days of this behavior during which time she was urged to lie back and let go, I whispered into her ear, "are you afraid to die now?" to which in a clear voice she responded, "yes, yes, yes!" I regret not having explored the fear that was in her before the nearly comatose period of terminality began. I have learned that a request for death does not necessarily mean that a terminally ill person is truly at peace and ready to die. But, the reverse of the statement, that no one can request death and mean it, is clearly not true, for many ill people do make peace and become quite ready to die. It is that we must be continuously vigilant not to accept as final a statement from any person that he wishes to die if this statement antecedes, even by only a day, that moment that brings one to the brink of death.

I have come to believe that the euthanasia under discussion is not always a peaceful concept of death but a flight from empty and useless suffering and as such, is more of a resignation in the face of oppression than a victory. The anxiety of suffering adds a critical brutality to the end of life. This anxiety may well come from a basic mistrust of the goodness of the world and a diminished sense of value of oneself. Undoubtedly there is an element of consideration for others. In some ways such consideration is warranted and blessed, for probably the best that there is to a life is its investment in the cause of others rather than only in self. Even a proximate death can have a meaning in the last remnant days of living if one feels safe in living. There are enough medications to ease the pain and anxieties of terminal life and there should be enough psychologic and social reason to give enhancement to the last flicker of life.

Nevertheless, the modern concept of euthanasia helps to force us, as a society, to look at life and the death belonging to it, and to ask what it is that we want of our deaths. Given choice, as we preach should exist for all major decisions in a man's life, how would an individual choose to die? What would he want of his death? To answer, one must have to understand what options are available and what supports exist or could be mobilized. We must also acknowledge that exchange of thought is important, that change and maturation of ideas will occur with time, and that we are all victimized by fantasies and projections. To understand our own death is to understand another's, to request something for ourselves is to implicitly acknowledge the needs of another. To search the question of our own death is to give new meaning to life and may well give vitality to the dying of our loved ones.

Psychoanalytically it may well be true that one cannot visualize oneself as dead, but such an explanation begs the question of confrontation of dying. We may stay inured and distant to the question until death of someone close occurs, but sooner or later it does happen and we are forced to confront intimately the terms of death. What we do with that initial confrontation may well permanently fashion our precepts for love, for understanding, for aging and for our own deaths.

The overriding issue is the legitimacy of death, death as part of life, dying of a person as part of that person's living, death as an instrument in the cosmic scheme of evolution, expansion, birth, growth, love, being. If we can perceive of a death as a natural part of each life, then we can begin to educate our children, our adolescents, our adults, our professionals and nonprofessionals as to the social and individualistic meaning of dying, of death, of loss and in some ways, of life itself. Such education can never eliminate the mystery and passion of death and that elimination certainly cannot be a legitimate goal for a society. But an education for death and dying can begin to ease the singular burden that most people must now face in silent confronting of fears, terrors and anguish finding little resourse for open discussion, except through disturbing humor or empty, high riding slogans.

Children come to understand death quite early in life although there is some argument as to what age the irreversibility of death is intellectually understood as applies to the self-person. Perhaps it is six years, perhaps nine. There is some indication that even younger children who develop a fatal illness, may have an extinction anxiety, an awareness in anxiety that their own personal, permanent death is close by. Regardless of the exact age of personal awareness in a youngster, he is constantly exposed to death themes in nursery rhymes, television cartoons, violence depicted in newspaper photos, and in listening to descriptions of events besetting the family, or in seeing and coming to know of tragedies in other families.

The child is constantly witnessing the death of animals, personal pets, strays, insects. He drives by cemeteries, funeral parlors, hospitals. Quite early in life many experiences come his way. These may terrify him or he may accept them peacefully, depending upon the attitudes of his family and other important people in his environment. The parent who insists that a cemetery is a park or playground, or who refuses to answer a child's question as to what dead is, in language that is pertinent and explicit for the intellectual resources of the child, may easily be transmitting an unmentionable and unbearable quality to the meaning of death that can initiate and promote great anxiety and turbulence in the growing child's affective and intellectual world. Anxieties in a parent are quickly and effectively transmitted to a child and became incorporated within the child's psyche.

Children need to feel that they are part of an ongoing, secure, belonging system. If death is portrayed as a discussable part of life, even though a part with mystery and sadness, the child is helped to master initiating anxieties and is given permission for further growth through discussion and sharing of feelings.

There is need to openly discuss feeling about death and loss in the nursery and grammar school. Most of our teachers are ill prepared to either discuss the topic as a neutral event or to take advantage of the opportunities presented through the death of a national figure, a grandparent or a pet, or to explore the physical meaning of death and the emotions aroused at the loss of a loved figure.

The classroom is a place where all manners of pain, betrayals and losses can be made part of the education of the child into a fuller and better humanity. The refusal or non-recognition of the opportunity for the teacher to deal with a pressing issue in the life of a student helps cement fantasy, withdrawal and loneliness for that child and can promote the creation of defensive shells that can easily distort later adult behavior in attempting to deal with unresolved anxiety. Oftentimes a teacher may recognize that something should be done in the classroom but feels embarrassed or inadequate to explore issues. Frequently the teacher imposes his or her own anxieties onto the class, inadvertently supporting children's inner fears and retreats. The improved training of teachers in this regard must be sought, and new directions in placing the themes of death, loss and suffering in general into the young child's learning directions explored.

Education if offered through many channels and certainly television has become a key instrument. Yet so little is done for children to help them master their fears at the time of a crisis. The assassinations of John and Robert Kennedy curtailed most scheduled programming as dirges and corteges and requiems filled network time. How little support was offered to children during those saddened moments. Misterogers, of repute in educational television, was perhaps the only children's programmer to attempt to create a vehicle for children, helping them to understand and share in the concerns, fears and horrors of violence and death. Yet children throughout the nation saw much, suffered much and probably bore the burden secretively within. Programs for parents and children alike about illness, aging, death and dying and mourning are much needed, but seldom available.

Many teenagers are beset with images and fantasies about death, causing a degree of discomfort and anxiety in daily living. During the past years I have had occasion to share in the thoughts of high school juniors and seniors in seminars about their thoughts of death. Several times I have been told of inner turmoil and fears related to the death of a sibling, parent or grandparent, these concerns resulting in a drop in scholastic performance, a turning away from pre-loss goals, a disquiet with life. Youngsters have talked of long periods of sleeplessness, of confusing dreams, of feelings of isolation and unreality. Some of these reactions may appear to be prolonged grief reactions and if so, may well be pathologic or bordering on the pathologic, in the sense that permanent damage to the psychologic and social character setting of the individual may be in the making, and could lead to serious psychiatric and/or social behavior disturbance in the future.

Simple discussion seminars are not therapeutic and should not be considered as such. They do, however, point to the need of both educating teachers to become responsive to the psychologic needs of a youngster when the death or loss of an important figure in their lives occurs, and to facilitating open discussions of the meaning of death as a regular classroom exercise. Several colleges have initiated seminars in "Death and Dying," conducted by interested faculty with various specialty backgrounds such as sociology, psychology, education and the like. There is need for a regular course in all schools, secondary as well as colleges. These courses and seminars must not be conceived as group therapy classes but nevertheless, it is essential that some sharing of individual anxieties and fears be encouraged.

For that very reason, teachers and seminar leaders must not be casual, or occasional, people or individuals attempting to explain to a class of young people how to overwhelm personal anguish by working through self-anxiety. A period of training for teachers in confronting human crises and anxieties should be required, set up by universities and colleges. Such training courses may easily be expanded to confrontation of crisis in any human loss spheres such as divorce, abandonment, moving from one residential area to another, etc. There may be a temptation in such education processes to either romanticize death, glorify dying or present concrete answers to human suffering, and all three motions must be scrupulously guarded against. An education in death and dying must be primarily directed toward viewing the problems with death in western society today, viewing personal and societal goals and ambitions devoted to easing the hurt and anguish of dying and loss, and allowing a personal confrontation with death to return to the group and to the society, as a problem meaningful for all.

Courses and seminars of any nature can stir up latent emotional confusion in an individual, and certainly education for dying and death may well arouse unresolved conflict. How does one talk of suicide to a young lady whose father committed suicide ten years ago? Can we talk of the meaning of suicide at any length without stirring great emotional tides in such a person? But we should not avoid the topic for that reason. What is needed is good backup support by well-trained psychiatrists, psychologists or ministers to assist such vulnerable people in more deeply working through latent or surfacing psychologic difficulties.

For the majority of young people who may not have suffered a deeply personal disturbance in a family death (and indeed, for most young people this is true today), exposure of ideas and feelings about death is just as pressing. Sooner or later, they too must confront death in a loved one, distant as he or she may be from intimate, youthful dependency. To understand the needs of the dying, to have some preparation for the communication, the support, the style, the manner, the pain of dying, is to facilitate helpful interrelation with a dying loved one and effect a more meaningful and proud goodbye-saying. To be educated to the nature of grief and bereavement is to be able to draw closer to the needs of the grieving, and to be helpful in the drawn out mourning that survivors must go through. And in the end, to have previously thought through and talked through some of the issues of dying and death, of aging and weakening, may prepare us all for an easier death.

An education forum for death and dying is not an answer to death. Religions, God, the cosmic, the transcendental have attempted to find some sort of answer to a personal death. These answers best subserve those who can use them. An education forum should certainly include modern religious thinking and contemporary cultural comparisons. Religion, humanism, sociology, biology may help us to understand the problems of the dying. Even though we may still hold ourselves to be singularly immortal, we need to be helped in mobilizing resources and supports for the other who is now dying. This by itself would be a great and important change from today's vacuum in the education of the needs of the dying. Compassion and consolation are essential elements of each man's humanism, professional or not. No one group and no one professional owns or possesses all the answers nor all the pretentions of knowing. Dying belongs to all men and love, compassion and helping must be confirmed as human conditions. It takes teaching, training, dialogues and exploration for each man to feel a competency in dealing with large human issues.

We are a professionalized society, but that does not mean that each citizen cannot be exposed to better ways of handling life's aches and tragedies. To trust blindly the professional, or the institution, robs us of an essential compact with life, for we need to promote and possess feelings of mastery, of competence, of courage, of style, when facing life's tribulations.

As long as men must die with no knowledge or certainty as to immortality or annihilation, fear and anxiety will exist. As long as taboos, dishonesties, fantasies, unapproachabilities and disorganizations exist, fear is accentuated and lonelines encouraged. To talk in common of the problems is to grow more comfortable with the human condition, and to feel comfort that what happens to one human may be the commonness of all humans. To be able to speak of guilt, of anger, of ambivalence, is not to free us of these affects, but in giving them public form, to promote the commonality of these feelings for all men and women. In the search for a peaceful death and indeed a more peaceful living and aging, how we educate ourselves towards fuller humanness will be reflected in how we live our lives.

1. Maslow, Abraham: *Toward a Psychology of Being.* New York, Van Nostrand Reinhold, 1968.
2. Lindemann, Erich: Symptomatology and management of acute grief.
(a) *American Journal of Psychiatry, 101*:141-148, 1944.
(b) Caplan, Gerald. *Principles of Preventive Psychiatry.* New York, Basic Books, 1964.